The
ORIGINAL
ART
of
MUSIC

Dorothy Ling

Published by
The Aspen Institute
and
University Press of America, Inc.

Library of Congress Cataloging–in–Publication Data

Ling, Dorothy.
The original art of music / Dorothy Ling.
p.   cm.
1. Music– –Philosophy and aesthetics. 2. Music and society.
I. Aspen Institute for Humanistic Studies. II. Title.
ML3800.L667   1988   88–19117 CIP
780'.1– –dc19
ISBN 0–8191–7117–4 (alk. paper).
ISBN 0–8191–7118–2 (pbk. : alk. paper)

Programs in the Arts

Philip F. Nelson
Director

From the beginning at Aspen, the humanistic tradition has always maintained a strong relationship between great books (the written tradition, centering on human reason) and great arts (the visual, aural, and oral traditions, which draw on the aesthetic and spiritual gifts that, together with reason, mark our human existence).

The Aspen Institute sponsors a range of programs in the arts including an active artists-in-residence program, whereby exceptionally talented young professional artists are invited to spend time at Aspen's Wye Center where they continue to develop their skills as artists. While the artists are in residence they share their special talents with the fellowship of The Aspen Institute and the residents of Maryland's Eastern Shore.

Additionally, the Arts Program of The Aspen Institute holds seminars in the arts and sponsors the publication of works which deal with the importance of the arts in each of our lives, and the enormous contributions the arts make in determining the sense of pride and worth a society has in itself.

A Program of The Aspen Institute
Wye Center, P.O. Box 222
Queenstown, Maryland 21658
(301) 827-7168

Contents

Introduction

Dorothy Ling's *The Original Art of Music* is the first in a planned series of monographs dealing with the arts to be published by The Aspen Institute as a part of its arts program at Wye Center.

It is intended that these publications will make available, for the first time, seminal works which represent important insights into the intrinsic relationships which exist between the arts and the individual and the arts and society. These relationships have always been of great concern in the humanistic tradition and to The Aspen Institute.

I became acquainted with Dorothy Ling and her remarkable work some years ago during my tenure as Dean of the Yale School of Music, and I was immediately impressed with the breadth and depth of her knowledge, professional background and, above all, by her extraordinary insights into the power of the arts in the educational process.

Dorothy Ling's life and work are based on the belief that the arts—all of the arts—inform *all* of school life, and that they are not to be treated as separate subjects. She believes that the purpose of artistic experience is to keep open or reopen the doors of perception. It is only through these doors that the channels of creativity, communication, imagination, and affection can operate to connect us with our innermost selves and with reality.

The remarkable influence for good of Dorothy's work, and that of her colleagues, is seen today in the fact that their schools have 450 students and 45 teachers; four primary schools, one high school, and one school for the training of teachers. An additional school opened in March of 1989. Also, teachers graduating from this year's class are starting a school in Patagonia.

What started as one kindergarten/primary school many years ago is now a complete system, including a training program for the education of their own teachers.

The Ministry of Education in Argentina, because of their interest in the original school, has funded one of the schools, bought the building for another, and will be helping with the funding of more new schools.

Yet, in spite of the school's obvious success, in the best sense of education, Dorothy Ling and Nelly Pearson (the co-founder and a teacher in the school) do not dwell on this growth. Rather, they feel that growth and numbers are always used as a way to tell the story of something which has succeeded. But they say it never entered their minds to do it for results. After all, there are innumerable efforts which can show hundreds of adepts, proliferation of entities and for all kinds of educational causes and ends. But they prove nothing. And Dorothy Ling does not want to be confused with those who work with such results in mind.

They do not want a story that tells of terrible efforts. It was no effort they say, it was not hard work, nor is now a reaping of it. It was what they did because they believed in it. That is the picture they want of the school. It would be against their whole philosophy to say, "See, this is what was achieved: 450 students, Ministry support, etc., etc." That is *not* success. That is *not* what they sought; but rather the moment in the classroom, in singing, in painting, in retelling a story or a history or the life of an insect. The numbers are not the results, only what happens in each child and in the teacher, and they are not computable or describable except in terms such as Dorothy's book attempts.

To my question about their results, Dorothy gave me quotes from *Ecclesiastes* which I share with you now:

> *To every thing there is a season, and a time to every purpose under the heaven.* (Chapter 3, Verse 1)

> *Whatsoever thy hand findeth to do, do it with thy might; for there is no work nor device, nor knowledge, nor wisdom, in the grave, whither thou goest.* (Chapter 9, Verse 10)

> *Cast thy bread upon thy waters; for thou shalt find it after many days.* (Chapter 11, Verse 1)

The narrative which follows is, then, both the story of a remarkable human being, and the chronicle of her search for the original art of music.

Philip F. Nelson
Vice President and Director
Programs in the Arts
The Aspen Institute
January, 1989

Preface

Everything knows something, and has some experience, and everything is a record of his own experience, knowledge and conditions are as convertible as force and heat. Their forms and qualities are the expression of this experience in so far as it has affected them.

— Samuel Butler *Notebooks*

The threshold of music is an invisible frontier or dividing line between the musical and unmusical. All thresholds are charged with symbolic implications. The threshold of music, although in itself manifest and self-evident, is nevertheless shrouded in mystery for most of us. It has taken me a lifetime of investigation to recover from what we might call a musical amnesia and rediscover it.

In the following pages, I mention only the different aspects of this research in terms of my own direct musical experience. I then bring to bear on it the studies of other investigators working mostly in fields other than music..

The reception and making of music is an inner individual experience which does not lend itself to scientific analysis. Here theory cannot replace experience; the road leads inwards not forwards. This inner search for what constitutes real music and real musicians is only comparable to the mythical hero's spiritual pilgrimage in search of himself and of truth. There is nothing new to be discovered, only that which always *was* and *is*. Excerpts from T. S. Eliot's *Four Quartets* (the revealing testimony of a pilgrim poet) will appear throughout this book as a kind of *leitmotif* illuminating the way.

And what there is to conquer
By strength and submission, has already been discovered
Once or twice, or several times, by men whom one cannot hope
To emulate—but there is no competition—
There is only the fight to recover what has been lost
And found and lost again and again: and now under conditions
That seem unpropitious. But perhaps neither gain nor loss.
For us there is only the trying. The rest is not our business.

— T. S. Eliot

Dorothy Ling
Buenos Aires, 1983

1   *The First Discovery*

When I graduated from Cambridge University and went with a scholarship to study Primitive Music under Professor E. von Hornbostel at the University of Berlin, I had excellent qualifications behind me and a promising future before me. I had been Turle Scholar and, as such, organist and choirmaster, at Girton College for three years. Two years later, however, when confronted with the question of specializing in some particular field of music, I was amazed to find there was none that aroused my interest and enthusiasm. I therefore retired from all musical activity for the next ten years during which I married a Spanish professor, and we moved to Spain to raise a family. We emigrated to England at the outset of the Civil War. There I was offered several interesting posts but was unable to accept them as, having married a foreigner, I was no longer a British subject. Three years later, in 1939, we moved to Argentina.

When I resumed my musical activity, it was at the University of Tucumán. Tucumán is a small provincial town, situated at the feet of the Andes, amongst vast sugar cane plantations and orange groves.

In the intervening lapse of ten years, I had had ample time to meditate upon the absurdity of my situation, for I had become a highly qualified specialist in an artistic language of which I was completely ignorant. I had no reason to blame my professors for this state of things. On the contrary, seeing that I had a certain musical facility, their task was more one of orientation than of actual teaching; in this they gave me the best of their knowledge, technique and human capacity. In spite of this, I realized that I had not the remotest idea of what music or a musician should be. My only chance of remedying this deficiency was to find out for myself, for the answers obtained from musicians of prestige were vague, misguiding and unsatisfactory.

I began by enumerating the principal constituents of music, only to find myself lost in a maze of enigmas for which I had no answers. Even at first glance, the complex nature of these elements was obvious:

Silence
Sound
Rhythm
Time
Space
Resonance
Audition
Expression
Imagination
Creativity
Affectivity

. . . a series of unknowns that my musical education had not resolved or even contemplated. Without a basic understanding of these elements and their *modus operandi* it was obviously impossible to cross the threshold of music.

In my passage through school, academy and universities, I had acquired a certain amount of information and knowledge of techniques for general application, which at this juncture only served to make the situation more obscure and confusing, whilst contributing nothing to the solution of the enigmas.

The mystery of the enigma and the labyrinth has always fired people's imaginations, inciting them to undertake the perilous voyage of the hero into the unknown, in search of the hidden treasure, the priceless pearl . . . that is, in search of truth, liberty and love. The vicissitudes and ordeals of this adventure are precisely those which will gradually transform them into authentic human beings and give them an understanding of themselves and of the universe, impossible to achieve by any other means.

An ancient myth reminds us that in order to find one's way out of the labyrinth, we need the help of Ariadne. To her I appealed, with apparently no success. But today, looking back over a lifelong pilgrimage, I am able to discern the firm orientation of her strong, subtle and invisible thread indicating, at the innumerable crossroads, "the straight and narrow way" to which the Holy Scriptures, Lao-Tse and wise men of all ages refer.

On this pilgrimage one must travel light, for the way is steep and rough. Faith is the only indispensable equipment, since every advance is a step in the dark, an incursion into unknown territory. On the way one receives strange gifts from the most unexpected sources, gifts of inestimable value; but it is not easy to recognize in them, at the time, the transcendental help without which the adventure would be desperate.

As you can only set out from where you are, I had to take my bearings to find out exactly where I stood. For me, it was evident that music, far from being a superfluous luxury (musical instruments are now classified as such by customs officers), was a vital necessity in man's daily life and prior to speech. This would seem to indicate that each and every one of us is born with a natural and spontaneous musical disposition, necessary to life. For this reason I had no faith in the general orthodox belief that music is something which has to be learnt, and consequently taught, in order to be valid. We don't teach a child to walk; we simply give it the necessary opportunity and encouragement.

The usual methods and orthodox approaches to music seemed to me to be totally inadequate. Furthermore, as far as I could judge, they were more concerned with the outer ear and eye, the intellect and techniques for general application, than with the musical ear, imagination, creativity and feeling. They did nothing to put those interested in music into direct live contact with musical experience. On the contrary, they imposed on him long years of previous learning and training, at once fatiguing and destructive . . . a kind of obstacle race ending with the correct reading and execution of the score of the so-called most difficult works, without ever crossing the threshold of music. Today it is possible to become a brilliant performer, composer or director without being a musician.

Many years later, in the belief that the university could, and should, be a natural ground for basic human orientation, I took the problem to various university authorities in Europe and

America. The only satisfactory reply came from the then Dean of the Yale School of Music, Professor Philip Nelson. He agreed with me as to the existence of a serious problem, striking at the very roots of human society. I asked him what he was able and willing to do about it. "Well," he said, "here at this School, all would-be professionals are furnished with all the elements and opportunities they need. Given moral and adequate financial support, they go ahead and do the rest for themselves. This leaves me free to concentrate on the situation of the hundreds of students studying other careers for whom a sustained musical activity, both individual and collective, is the breath of life. I feel it is my responsibility to give them every facility for this activity. And thus far, this is the most I have been able to do."

2   *A Fresh Start*

I had by now formed a general idea of what was ineffec-
tual and absurd in musical activity, but my convictions had
necessarily to be put to the test in daily musical experience, and
more specifically in the realm of teaching, where I felt that nothing should be taught, only discovered.

By a strange coincidence, it was at this precise moment
that the University of Tucumán appointed me to reorganize the
teaching of music in an experimental school and college run
under its auspices, the Escuela y Liceo Vocacional Sarmiento. This
appointment was a godsend which provided me with a field of
action by no-action for the next sixteen years.

What I proposed to do, was simply to rouse and mobilize
in all students, without distinction or exception, their innate
capacity to make music, to awaken in them a spontaneous desire
to sing, and give them the opportunity to do so, free of all the
restraints of knowledge and technique.

Voices were never selected—such a thing would have
been absurd. The important thing was that everybody should
sing, in or out of tune, with such a voice as they had, whether in
class or in public. We began by singing in unison, and I was
surprised to find how soon everyone was singing expressively
and in tune. My task was to give them the opportunity of discovering the joy of making music by participating in my own delight.

The musical material employed was always authentic
musical value . . . national and international folksongs, medieval
songs, arias, and polyphonic works by classical composers. I
chose a wide variety, knowing that this vocal music, absorbed
and sung by ear would provide pupils with an inner flow of
melodies which would accompany them at all times, a kind of

"manna" which would nourish and sustain them in the desert places of life.

All music was approached by ear, without the use of scores. These were introduced later, when students enjoyed discovering in writing what they were joyfully singing by ear.

Amongst other things, I invited my pupils, whose ages ranged from seven to eighteen, to make their own songs, offering them texts of true poetic content to choose from. It was a revealing experience for all concerned. In those days there were no tape recorders in Tucumán, so the children had to wait in line for me to take down their song at dictation, something I could do with rapidity. But even so, the majority of the children had created and forgotten a dozen songs before their turn came. I participated in this creative play by bringing to light the latent accompaniment implicit in the songs.

These were immediately put into circulation anonymously, thus passing into folksong, for what is folksong but the spontaneous creation of those who take joy in singing? Eventually the university published some of them in two volumes. They are still in circulation and are a live testimony to the paralysis and waste of creativity produced by orthodox methods. A child who has once made his own song (a thing all children do spontaneously before going to school) knows he can always do it at will.

By then I had been appointed professor of music at the University Instituto de Educación Física, where young men and women were preparing to become teachers. I was in charge of their musical education. This post, which I held for several years, enabled me to discover many important things.

One of the first things to make a deep impression on me was the fact that physical training was organized basically on a 2/4 or 4/4 rhythm. The physical deformity which this unilateral accentuation provoked was painfully evident: an inclination of the body through its weight falling predominantly on one side of it, and an uneven muscle development. I therefore set myself to observing people walking on the streets, and great was my surprise to discover that it was really exceptional to find someone moving to a rhythm of 3/4. I sent out my students to make their own observations and they confirmed my own. I then proceeded to observe the movements of my own students, and I found that of a group of thirty-five, only one or two had a 3/4 rhythm. These were often those whose vital intelligence was superior to their intellectual development and achievement, and therefore they were not ranked among the best students.

I was intrigued by this discovery which became my standard test for examining each new group of students. Studying this phenomenon for my own interest, I began to feel that to walk naturally in a 3/4 rhythm might possibly be a foretaste of a liberation from duality and gravity, for the force of gravity is felt to be much less when moving in 3/4, than in 2/4. From what I was able to observe, the 3/4 rhythm is not constant, only predominant. In states of fatigue, worry or physical disorder, it relapses into 2/4, and you feel your feet dragging. If in such circumstances one remembers to impose a 3/4 movement, the relief and improvement one experiences is very real and almost immediate. One of my students, on the day she graduated, confided to me that one of the really important things she had learnt during her career, was that physical education should be organized on a basic rhythm of 3/4, not 2/4 and that she proposed to remedy this situation in her future work.

The basis of these students' work with me was first singing, and secondly, to acquire the ability to let music dictate their movements instead of them imposing pre-established movements on the music. On one occasion, and as a final examination, I asked my students to recreate amongst themselves a French folkdance which was unknown to them, by just allowing the music to control their movements and thus indicate to them the corresponding steps and figures. It was amazing to see how, after a few minutes, the precise movements and figures of the dance suddenly began to emerge out of the chaos. Everyone was dancing, full of the joy of a creative experience.

3 *"Romances"*

The first unexpected gift I received was from a young couple of Spanish artists, Antonia Calderón y José Jordá, actors, singers and dancers, who had been disciples and intimate friends of Garcia Lorca. They passed through Tucumán on their way back to Buenos Aires after an artistic tour of Latin America. They had undertaken this trip after Margarita Xirgu's theatrical company, which had brought them to America, was dissolved at the outset of the Spanish Civil War. The Philharmonic Society of Tucumán had asked them for a recital of Spanish folksongs and dances. A day's sojourn extended to a month owing to a public demand for more recitals. I had the good fortune to be their accompanist.

Living and working with them for a whole month was a most revealing and unforgettable experience. I was greatly impressed by a strange impersonal affectivity and transparent innocence which flowed incessantly through everything they sang, and produced a profound resonance in their audiences. They seemed to *be* the music. They, in turn, having had to make do with poor or indifferent accompanists all over South America, were surprised to find that, although English, I was able to play the songs as if I had been born in each of the Spanish regions from which they came.

I was married to an eminent Spanish philologist and investigator, Clemente Hernando Balmori, and had lived in Spain for six years, but knew only two of the regions in question, and had never engaged in any musical activity whilst living in the peninsula. It was no easy task for any musician to produce at a moment's notice the infinite variety of rhythms and styles which characterize Spanish folksongs. The only chance I had of being able to respond to such an exigency was just to let the music play me. The result seemed to be pure magic. When the time for parting came, this young couple and I had become life-long friends. This was somewhere around 1944. My friends are still living and working and in spite of a lifetime of intense artistic activity, fraught with innumerable difficulties, their work has lost none of its transparency, affectivity and innocence.

As a legacy, they left me a copy of all the musical material they possessed and which they themselves had collected in Spain. As time passed, this legacy increased and multiplied with the addition of material found by me.

Of all their repertory, the songs that most impressed me and their audiences were the old "romances." Their texts are usually studied and analyzed in classes on Spanish literature, but never sung. Worse still, the texts and music of these romances have been collected by the separate groups of investigators, with the result that texts and music were published in separate volumes.

It was very strange to see the effect these old romances invariably produced, even in the most sophisticated audiences. A sepulchral silence and a profound nostalgia seemed to invade them. It is with this material that rural communities have always nourished and educated the younger generations . . . an oral tradition, of great mythic content, firmly sustained over the centuries.

Many years later, I found a reference to these romances in Mircea Eliade's *Images and Symbols*. Referring to their eternal validity and efficacy, he says: "The most terrible historical crisis of the modern world—the Second World War—all it brought with it and generated—has served to demonstrate that the extirpation of myths and symbols is a mere illusion. Even in the most desperate historical situations, such as the trenches of Stalingrad or in the the Nazi or Russian concentration camps, men and women sang these old songs and listened to narrations, even sacrificing part of their meagre rations to be able to do so. These old songs and stories reactualized the myths and were charged with nostalgia. All that essential part of man which we call 'imagination' swims in a sea of symbolism and continues to feed on archaic mythologies and theologies."

In W. H. Hudson's *Green Mansions* one of the characters remarks: "It seemed to me on that evening that my feelings could be adequately expressed only in that sublimated language used by the finest minds in their inspired moments; and accordingly I fell to reciting. But not from any modern, nor from the poets of the last century, nor even from the greater seventeenth century. I kept to the more ancient romances and ballads, the sweet old verse that, whether glad or sorrowful seemed always natural and spontaneous as the song of a bird and so simple that even a child can understand it."

These romances still remain a basic material for all my work. It was they that brought me a second unexpected gift. My doctor, on learning of my interest in old romances obtained a special permission for me to visit a closed community of Sephardic Jews to whom he gave medical assistance. They held him in high esteem for having saved the lives of several of them. Many worked as greengrocers, and all lived together as a community in a spacious old colonial house, still attractive in spite of its ruinous condition. Most of them were from the Near East.

When my doctor took me along to the house one day after working hours, all the adults came into the principal courtyard or "patio" with the solemnity of those who are about to participate in some traditional rite . . . about thirty people in all. They all spoke the old medieval Spanish and some still held in their possession an enormous key to their former houses in Toledo. They sat down in a circle and their cantor, or official singer, appeared. He was a young fisherman who had escaped to South America to avoid military service under the Turkish government. He began to sing an old sephardic romance which seemed to have a great musical affinity with the old Gregorian plainchant.

I had permission to take down the music and the texts, but when I disposed to do so, I realized that tears were flowing silently down the faces of all those present, and I joined in this ritual lament for paradise lost. Afterwards I was able to jot down several romances, although with a feeling of sacrilege. When I left, I thanked them for having allowed me to participate in such an intimate experience.

4 *The Musical Image and Meaning*

Towards the end of the forties, I received another gift, which kept me intensely occupied for the next ten years. A friend sent me a copy of a review edited by ICANA (Instituto Cultural Norteamericano), drawing my attention to one of the articles it contained. Written by a North American school teacher, it told of the work she had done with her pupils in an attempt to discover the nature of the relation between the visual arts and music. Having studied the article, I was fully convinced that both the approach to the matter and the conclusions drawn were erroneous. But it posed a serious question. If this was the wrong answer, what would the correct one be? Could what music transmitted be made visible?

My response to musical stimuli is dynamic. I realized that this response could be made visible if I held a pencil in my hand and allowed it to leave traces on paper. Music came to me as a rhythmic flow of sound articulated into meaningful units or phrases. Pencil in hand and listening interiorly to a phrase from some known work, I allowed my simultaneous response to leave traces on paper. The result was a continuous unbroken line which began and ended with the music. This meant that it had necessarily been drawn speedily, thus precluding the possibility of intellectual reflection and intervention on my part.

Imagine my surprise and consternation when I found my response to be a formless, senseless scribble. I was totally disconcerted. If, by an analogous process of inner obedience to musical stimuli, I had been able to recreate the characteristic rhythms and atmosphere of Spanish folksongs which were completely unknown to me, what was happening now?

I became so intrigued and involved in this problem that I spent months, and eventually years, insisting on this test, working with different themes. At last the page began to clear, as the sky after a storm. My response continued to be amorphous but less chaotic. Something urged and incited me to continue; I had the feeling that behind this veil was hidden the clue to my enigmas. So I worked intensely for ten years. It soon became evident that everything depended on the degree and quality of my obedience to the demands of the music. During these years I worked not only with music but also with poetry which is likewise a flow of sound articulated into units of meaning which do not arise out of the words as such.

This was and continues to be one of the most fertile and fascinating experiences of all the various aspects of my research, for it was thus I learned to discriminate clearly between the different levels of interior attention and obedience. In the course of my work, these levels appeared in the following order:

1. Scribble
2. Scribble, but less chaotic
3. Incipient form
4. Meaningless form
5. Aesthetic form
6. Symbolic, meaningful form

When at last I was able to penetrate to the level of form, I saw that every time I used the same theme, a different form resulted. Not even I, who had drawn them, was able to repeat the forms which appeared at the sixth level.

Many years of intense work produced a series of drawings at the sixth level which greatly impressed me and others who saw them, although we know not why. The time had now come for me to find out more about them.. I had planned to take some of my work to Buenos Aires and make inquiries there, but the director of the Instituto Británico, who had taken an interest in my experience, advised me to await the imminent arrival of the Representative of the British Council. I showed him my collection of drawings, playing him the musical theme that had given rise to each one. Having received them with great attention and in silence, he then said: "I don't profess to have any knowledge of this subject; my field is classical languages. All I can say is that it is many years now since I received such a strong impression. The last time was in Turkey, when I saw the Dervishes dance for the first time. But I am sure my wife will be able to tell you more about it. Come and visit us." I naturally accepted his invitation.

My encounter with his wife, Constance Macnab, was extremely fruitful and orienting. She was a well-known Hungarian writer who, as a diplomat's daughter, had lived in many countries and spoke and wrote fluently in many languages. She was also a painter and a sculptress. She had spent many years in the Near East absorbing its ancient wisdom and philosophies. She had worked for many years with Ouspensky, the Russian mathematician and psychologist, and was also a close friend of T.S. Eliot. It was she who opened for me the door to the meaningful world of symbols, of which I knew nothing. She also introduced me to *The Four Quartets* of T.S. Eliot. I was thus able to discover the symbolic content of my drawings. This made me realize that when I responded adequately to the impact of artistic sound images, dynamic symbolic forms would build up inside me to convey wordless meaning and make me *be* the music. I have included some of these drawings on the following pages representing expressive form inherent in music and poetry. I have also indicated their origin.

Kyrie Eleison
B minor Mass
J.S. Bach

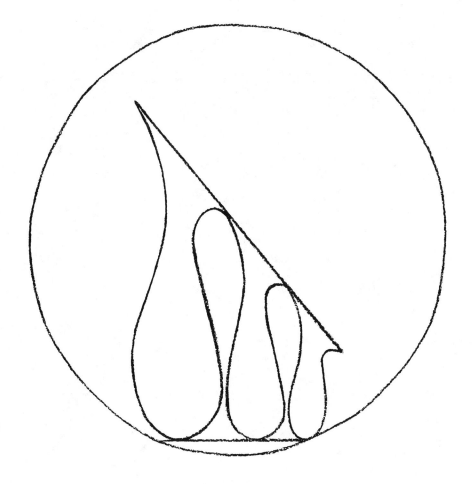

Ve — ni   Cre — a — tor   Spi — ti — tus

Liber Antiphonarius – *In festo Pentecostes*

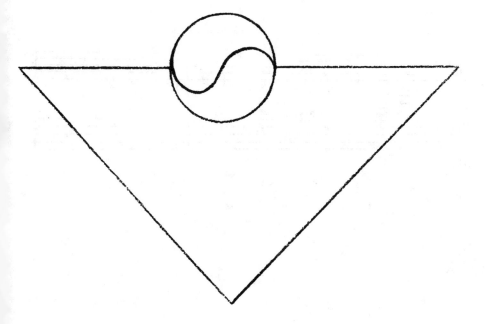

Ein' Feste Burg
J.S. Bach

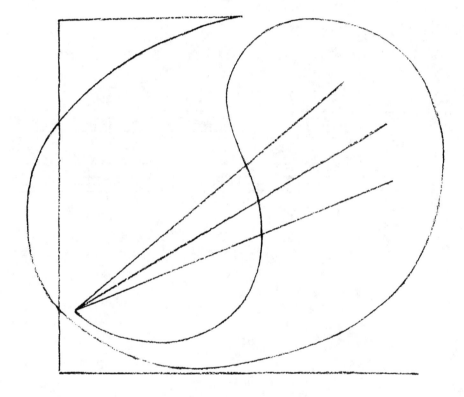

The prophet bird
Schumann – Op. 82-No. 7

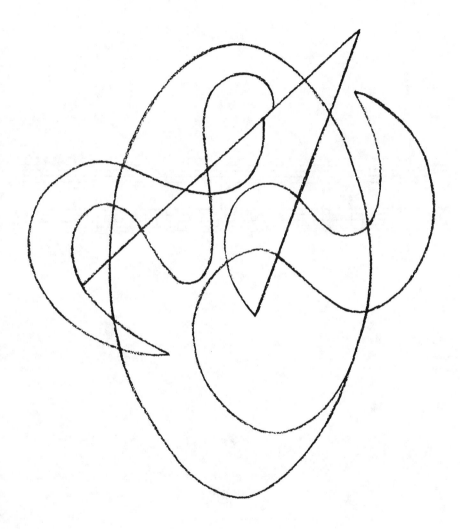

Prelude No. 15-Op. 28
Chopin

Chacarera
Argentine folksong

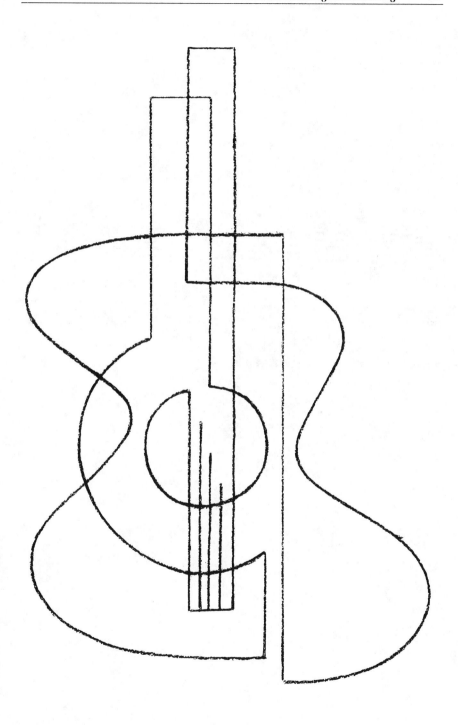

Requiem
J. Brahms

The blue deep thou wingest,
And singing still dost soar, and soaring ever singest.

—Shelley *Ode to a Skylark*

And every tongue, through utter drought,
Was withered at the root.
We could not speak, no more than if
We had been choked with soot.

—Coleridge *The Ancient Mariner*

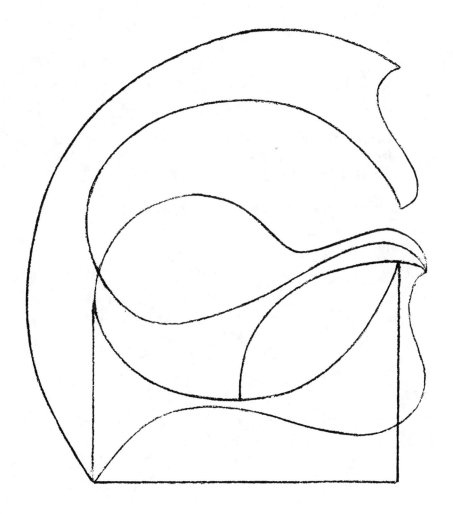

Her coat that with the tortoise vies,
Her ears of jet and emerald eyes
She saw and purred applause.

—Gray *On a Favorite Cat*

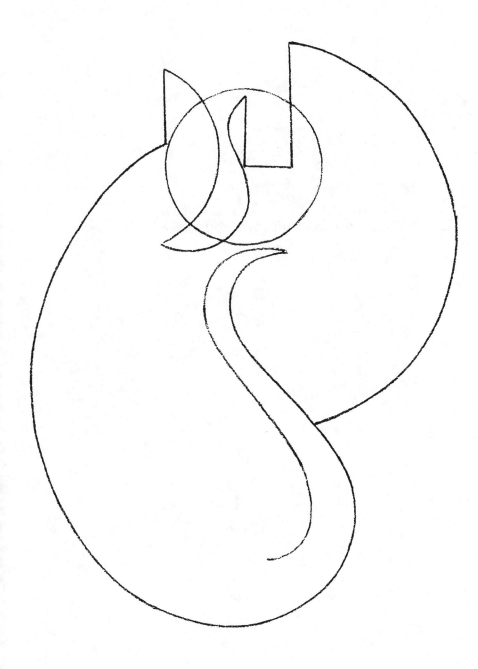

When I consider how my light is spent
'Ere half my days in this dark world and wide.

—Milton *On His Blindness*

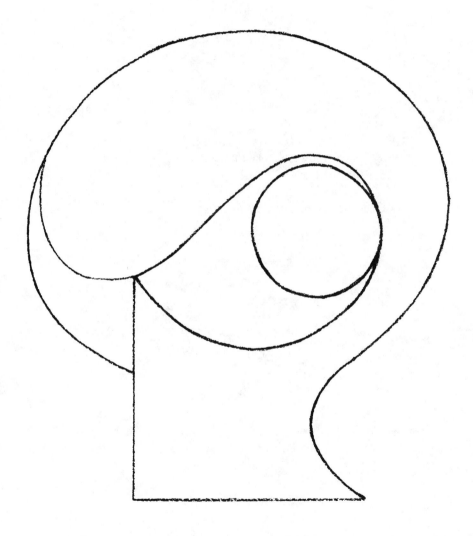

Why look'st thou so? – With my crossbow
I shot the albatross.

—Coleridge *The Ancient Mariner*

But to apprehend
The point of intersection of the timeless
With time, is an occupation for the saint.

—T.S. Eliot *The Four Quartets*

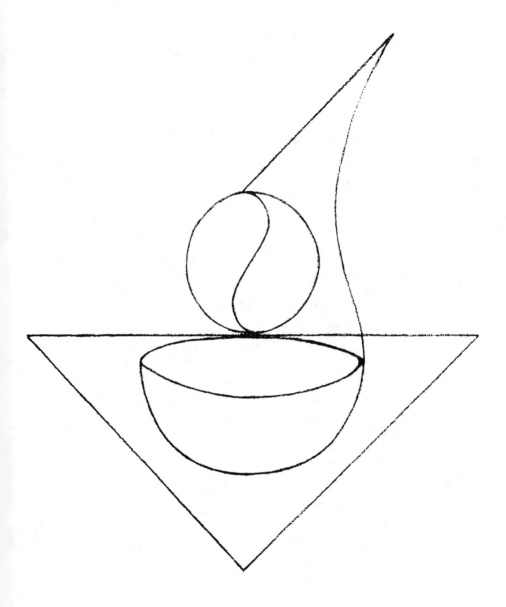

5 *University Teaching*

In 1955, I moved with my family from Tucumán to La Plata. There, at the local university, I was for many years in charge of the teachers' training course for students graduating in music from the Escuela de Bellas Artes. For several years I held the same post at the Universidad del Litoral in Rosario.

I now had to deal with university students. To them I proposed the old enigmas of music which were still unsolved, inviting them to accompany me in my search for the right answers (as vital for them as for me). All research was done through direct musical experience and not by theorizing. The basis for this was always singing and for this we used folksong and classical music of all periods.

I felt that the time was now ripe for us to incorporate into our own experience the ample spectrum of that of others, for I had realized that in fields outside music there existed a live interest in the phenomenon of music . . . far more perhaps than in the field of music itself. We explored studies which bore witness to a similar concern for the same enigmas. These were always put to the test in direct musical experience, since there is no understanding without experience. Some of these studies will later be cited at length.

The regular students who came to me were in their last year, and most of them were so weary and bored with ten years' previous training in theory and technique, repeating exercises and accumulating information, that many of them had long since forgotten their initial love of music and were now only interested in their career and in graduating as soon as possible. To work with me implied setting off on a new track from the very beginning. Only a minority were able to see this as a real opportunity and make the most of it. Not so the students who came as listeners who weren't taking the class for a grade. They had not come in search of a career, but moved by a vital interest in finding an orientation which would give form and meaning to their daily lives. All those who set off with me then on a voyage of exploration and have continued to advance in the same direction, whatever the cost, are still my fellow travelers, visible or invisible. To them I am indebted for innumerable and priceless original accounts of their own experiences on the way.

The basis of our work is an audible and inaudible dialogue between equals. It was one of my free students who, during the first class he attended, took out pen and paper and began to write at furious speed. At the end of the class he handed me the paper. It said:

> The disciple is a part and the whole of an act of induction to an opening up of oneself, after which the master is no longer master, nor the disciple, disciple.
>
> *the master is a reed*
> *the disciple cascade*
>
> *the master is life*
> *the disciple soul*
>
> *the master is a rose*
> *the disciple mallow*
>
> *the master is night*
> *the disciple dawn*
>
> *the master is omega*
> *the disciple alpha*
>
> *the master is everything*
> *the disciple is nothing.*
>
> — Carlos Riera Cervantes (free translation)

The regular students began to discover that in the way they had been trained, they had partially developed their outer ear, but nothing had been done to develop their inner musical ear, which meant that they were musically deaf. The sounds they produced vocally, or on their instruments, were mostly opaque and aggressive and therefore incapable of transmitting anything, for this type of sound is not adequate for musical purposes. Worse still, for many years they had allowed the eye to substitute for the ear. They were unable to discern what was music and what was not. It was no easy task for me, or for them, to find an oasis in this desert. This was their last year of study and the time lapse was obviously insufficient for them to be able to abandon a world of illusion and accede to reality.

6   *The Music Workshop*

When I retired in 1965, I decided to continue my work at home. I was now free of all academic demands. So I set up a music workshop which would allow me to widen my experience. Many of my university students participated, forming a nucleus into which newcomers were incorporated. These latter were not music students, but people interested in orienting themselves through the experience of music. Participation in the workshop was by invitation or request and restricted to those over twenty-one. Only those sincerely interested in their own development were admitted. The resulting group of people was richly heterogeneous; besides being of different cultural and ethnic backgrounds, there were those who could sing in tune or read music and those who could not. It was also kaleidoscopic, for hundreds of young people passed through, but only a minority persisted. However, those who withdrew took with them an experience which would serve as a point of reference for future orientation.

No rules were laid down, no organization imposed. And, most important of all, no one directed the workshop. Each individual coming into the workshop was in a unique life situation known only to himself. No personal inquiries were made either then or at any other time, but everyone engaged in impersonal dialogue with others at any time. Dialogue for us was not conversation or discussion; it was a mutual convocation on the level of being.

We gathered on weekends at my apartment in Buenos Aires. Everyone was free to dispose of his time as he felt inclined, but we all came together for two hours for singing and for the reading of some relevant text, such as those which are cited in this book. When texts were read, they were not discussed, nor were

any comments made, since the text would naturally set up different resonances, if any, in each one of us, according to his immediate interests and needs. We also came together for meals, pre-
pared by anyone so disposed. Breaking bread together was felt to
be an invisible ritual. Musical experience was what held us and
our activities together. Some of us already played a musical
instrument; the rest soon learnt to play guitar or recorder.

Our first concern with regard to musical experience was
the production of musical sound—resonant, expressive, buoyant,
and transparent. This can only be obtained by turning one's
attention inwards and making of oneself a resonator. This we
gradually achieved by coming out of prolonged silence through
humming into effortless singing which was always directed
inwards towards oneself. To increase the volume of sound we
increased the resonance not the intensity. If the voice is directed
outwards and force is used, the result is an unmusical, opaque,
earthbound sound which cannot transmit anything.

Our second concern was that everyone, in developing his
capacity to produce musical sound, should find his real natural
voice. Most people use acquired voices, not their own. The next
step was singing expressively in unison, with no one conducting,
which requires inner attention and obedience. We thus came
naturally into the experience of freedom through inner obedience.
This experience was then carried over into the singing of polyphonic music, where everyone is singing a different song with
expressive freedom, but in strict obedience to the demands of the
music.

The rhythmic-expressive unity which results from this
brings the music to life by transmitting significant sound images.
The quality of the voices is ethereal, as if raised in prayer. As
everyone's attention is turned inwards and expressively raised to
the level of being, a real communication is established between
the singers themselves and also with anyone listening, and all experience a joy of living.

This musical experience of freedom to express oneself
through inner obedience, communication, and joy of living had
then to be carried over into everyday life by sustaining this same
attitude for all our activities. There should be no fundamental
difference, in this sense, between singing, playing, sweeping the

floor, or washing dishes. We usually change our attitude with every change of activity, and everything is of differing importance. Thus it is that we are left with very few activities, if any, capable of producing in us a joy of living, or allowing us to communicate with our fellow beings.

The task of dealing with the contingencies of everyday life from a single musical attitude meant, of course, that most of the real work was done outside the workshop. Gathering at weekends simply activated and reinforced it. It required a sincerely sustained effort; the combined pressure of everybody's work on themselves was very high and rose subtly from one week to the next. This process of transformation compelled us to contemplate each other always as if for the first and last time. It was no longer possible to catalogue anyone for all time, as we are accustomed to doing.

As everyone had a voice with which to sing, we were able to sing a great variety of monodic and polyphonic music with the participation of all present.

At one time we decided to amplify our experience by singing in public in some of the important concert halls in Buenos Aires and the provinces—always as a means of investigation. The works we sang were never rehearsed (in the professional sense of the word), corrected or directed. The music was sung frequently and as a whole, but always as if for the first and only time, each one assuming the responsibility for his participation and giving of his utmost expressive capacity. Often we put away a work for several weeks during which time it always improved, because our inner musical capacity had improved, through inner attention.

When singing in public, our programs always included what are professionally known as difficult or complex works (amongst ourselves we made no such distinctions). It is usual for performers to feel a certain nervous expectation and uncertainty immediately before and during a concern. We had always wondered why we felt so free and easy, so full of calm assurance in these situations. I now feel that this can only be attributed to the fact that our whole attention was directed inwards towards a mythical level of being, not concerned with performance but with the experience being the music.

I was fully convinced that artistic expression, whatever form it assumed, was a free, intimate and unique manifestation of each individual and therefore could not be directed. Singing in public proved to be a most rewarding experience, for it allowed us to make several observations. For instance, if, as was often the case, we made an error, as long as we maintained the rhythmic flow of sound images, no interruption occurred and the fact passed unnoticed. Then too, we found that our audiences always reacted in the same way. They participated in the music in such a way as to obliterate the score and the singers and be left with a strange sense of plentitude, peace, joy and freedom. After the concert, all commentaries were to this effect and not on us or the music.

On one occasion when we sang Byrd's five-part *Mass* and Christmas music in the cathedral of Santa Rosa, a blind man sitting beside the bishop said to him: "Monseñor, if it is possible to hear such voices on earth, what shall we not be able to hear in Heaven?" On another occasion, singing in Tucumán, the organizers of the concert were so intrigued by the feeling of well-being which our mode of singing had produced in them that they invited us to stay on for a week, housed with different families, because they wanted to see whether the freedom of action, mutual understanding and joy of living they had perceived on the concert platform could be achieved and maintained by us amidst the ordinary difficulties of daily life.

Another revealing experience was working on a tapestry. We chose the Bayeux Tapestry because it was originally made by a large group of children and adults. Our intention was not to reproduce the tapestry but to reactualize it as a means of meditation. What was valuable to us was not the product but the experience. Work had to be done in absolute silence, for as soon as anyone began talking, the whole situation changed from one of spiritual meditation to a chattering sewing class. Forty people of all ages participated, but the resulting tapestry appeared to have been made by a single person.

It became desirable for us to venture into painting, theatre, foreign languages and popular music in order to amplify our field of observation and experience. We also acquired a piece of land, up in the mountains of Córdoba, with the idea of constructing a rudimentary shelter which would enable us to continue our work during the summer holidays. The ground was stony, treeless and waterless. Our idea was to start from zero and put to the test our capacity to live and work together in harmony and mutual understanding under the most adverse and precarious circumstances, in the same leaderless way in which we sang.

7   *Educational Research*

We had by this time initiated a Centro de Investigación Pedagógica. The idea of creating an Institute for educational research centering on a school for young children arose naturally out of my university teaching. My students and I were seriously engaged in discovering what the making of true music and musicianship required of us. In so doing, we realized that our customary attitudes, gestures, and scale of values had all been acquired. Of our total mental potentiality only one aspect, the rational, had been seriously contemplated by schooling. Even the teaching of art and music had been rationalized. Such things as emotion, intuition, imagination, myth, originality, spontaneity, freedom of expression, creativity, and affectivity had not been considered matters of prime importance.

Two of my students and I were especially interested in attempting a process of education for young children, to begin at a very early age, which would modify this situation. One of these students placed a large room of her house at our disposal, and after several unsuccessful attempts, the school began.

It seemed important to us all to attempt to keep alive, and prolong into adolescence, the young child's capacity for imaginative play, the creation and reception of artistic images, their cosmic vision of totality and the mythical landscape of their existence. This could only be achieved by the use of artistic images in the hands of creative adults interested in self-knowledge and development. A close contact with young children gives one a very clear point of reference for measuring the ravages that time and living in an utilitarian society have wrought in us.

We estimated that the experience of a childhood spent creatively in the company of their brothers and sisters, other children, and creative adults should give children a point of reference by which to orient themselves at any moment of their lives. They would know, from experience, that the mode of life modern society offers them is not the only possibility, and that there exists another, much more significant and fulfilling, which is not utopian, and which, at a critical stage of their existence, had brought them happiness and adventure.

We began with two teachers and two pupils, and the institution has survived for over twenty-two years. At present we work with children from three to thirteen, but we also tried the experiment of taking them at the age of two, for we found that the most decisive period of a child's education was up to the age of five, for by this time, if adequate care is lacking, children have already succumbed to the increasing pressure of an adult materialized world and have been uprooted from their first world and its characteristic gestures and attitudes. We now have fourteen teachers and a hundred children. No teacher is full-time; they earn their livings elsewhere. The Institute is private and pupils pay a modest sum. All necessary material is provided by the school in order to assure its good quality. Teachers receive a small subsidy to cover their expenses, and the rest is invested in maintenance and equipment. No one owns or directs the Institute. It is everyone's responsibility. All children attending the school must be followed by their brothers and sisters in order to avoid conflicts and confusion in the home.

All the children spend a five-hour day in a large glass-walled room, looking out on a well-kept garden planted with flowers, flowering trees and shrubs. The children use this garden for playing and climbing trees, but they and their teachers are all responsible for its upkeep. Everyone participates in all the aspects and phases of gardening, thus acquiring a sustained basic experience of Nature both physically and emotionally.

There are two other rooms, one for arts and crafts, and another for music and slide and film projection. There is also a kitchen and an office for receiving parents. In general, all the children work simultaneously in the large room divided into small groups which sit in circles on floormats. At the end of the day, after cleaning up the premises, they all sit in silence in one large circle to break bread together (they are served two crackers or cookies) and afterwards sing together in unison, for twenty minutes, folksongs and romances, to the accompaniment of guitars. The circle is a very powerful symbolic image, creating a sense of unity and totality. It is the basis of many traditional children's games. What impresses us daily is the vision and the experience of sitting in a circle with a hundred children, aged three to thirteen, and a few teachers, in complete silence for ten minutes. On occasions I have seen them sit in silence for twenty minutes or half an hour. The silence is produced by mutual consent, not by rigid enforcement, and becomes an essential part of daily life.

The children are not taught in the scholastic sense we usually attach to the word, but induced by the presentation of suitable material and relevant experiences to discover things for themselves. They then make their own written version, mostly illustrated, of what they have been working on. For illustrating, they use oil pastels and never draw objects, but create images. They learn to read and write at a very early age—the basic gestures of writing are developed with the aid of singing. Vocabulary is introduced by the association of the word or the idea with an artistic image. At first they read only the texts of the many songs they know by heart—the children's first reading books are collections of stories which they have themselves created and illustrated.

The basic material used in all fields of interest (which are considered as one) is the artistic image. The children neither study nor memorize, as it is unnecessary. What one experiences through the impact of artistic images is not easily forgotten and links up everything together, in such a way that one thing recalls another. Maps are drawn with great facility as artistic images, whilst being approximately accurate.

Between the ages of three and five, they are familiarized (through images, drawing and painting) with the basic organization of the universe, both on a macro and a microscopic level . . . from galaxies to atoms, cells and molecules—and also with how life is generated and maintained.

Myth, legend and folktales are used extensively, and storytelling passes naturally at a later stage into the reading of original documents and well-written narratives of travelers, explorers, investigators, historians and literary writers, thus keeping alive oral tradition. This is complemented by the projection of slides and documentary films. The children have at their disposal a small but very selected reference and circulating library. University research workers are occasionally invited to talk to the children about their work. Sometimes the children themselves offer to give a class. Generally speaking, they think of a class as storytelling or narration or as a display of material to be examined. For instance, one very young child said his father, who was a doctor, had a bag of old bones which he could lend him. Along he came next day with his bag of bones. These he produced and passed around from hand to hand amongst his group, children of his own age. The bones were then laid out on the tiled floor and set in order by an adult teacher to form a human skeleton. Each child chalked an outline of one of the bones and each was given its scientific name. Some bones were missing, but these were drawn in and named. The children had great fun finding these bones in their own and other children's bodies. They then made a paper model, fitted it together, and strung it up for everyone to see.

Drawing and painting are part of their daily life. The younger ones do so naturally without any stimulus. The older ones are often presented with a reproduction taken from the field of art (from pre-historic to modern) as a stimulant. They never copy it; they just recreate and reactualize it. This experience gives them a far greater understanding of the history of art than any technical, explanatory information, which is never offered. They also work in tapestry and clay modelling.

We cover the entire official school program, but it is worked through creatively, through artistic imagery. Great stress is laid on the quality of all material and elements present in the school.

The best description of our school came from a boy who had passed on into ordinary high school and was in his first year. He was a born storyteller and used to hold his collegemates spellbound with the mythical science fiction tales he told. They all wanted to know where and how he had learnt of so many interesting things, he being so young. "Well," he said, "I went to a school that wasn't a school, where the teachers knew nothing and taught you nothing, and where we didn't have to learn anything."

As the ancient Athenians well knew, this kind of essential creative education through participation can only be realized on the basis of small units. It cannot be mass-produced through official measures however well-intentioned. The intention of this educational activity, which covers all the normal school requirements, is to strengthen and develop in the child the scale of values and the vision of life pertaining to his first world so that he will not abandon them under adult pressure. We are especially interested in preserving his natural capacity for the perception of gesture and image which underlie actions and objects. Through the medium of the exemplary creative gestures of the teachers and a permanent creative activity, we attempt to mobilize, strengthen and vivify the child's innate wisdom, so that he may be able to resist the amnesia which our adult society induces in him in every possible way. To be a teacher in this school requires a right attitude and a sincere interest in self-development; the Institute is as much a school for teachers as for children. The teachers' basic task is to create, by their presence and attitude, a sacred space for living and working together. As we shall see later, sacred space has no ecclesiastical connotations. It refers simply to the quality of an unpolluted ontological space as vital to the well being of the spirit as unpolluted air and water are to the body.

Until the end of 1983, the year in which the first draft of this book was written, we carried on our work as a private enterprise, the children paying a modest sum for their education. But in 1984, at the request of the Ministry of Education, we initiated the same experiment for them, but extending it to include high school and an Institute for the training of teachers to be educators, not instructors, in a three-year course at university level. As our staff was totally insufficient to sustain two parallel experiments, we transferred ourselves to the Ministry, on condition that they gave us a free hand. They agreed, and promised us a new building which is now under construction. Education is now free.

The first group of educators graduated in 1986, and in 1987 one of them opened a new school for children of three to thirteen, a few miles away, assisted by third year students. The remaining graduates were absorbed by us. Our intention is to open a new school every year in this way. In 1988 we shall probably be opening two new schools: one in the extreme south of the country, in Ushuaia, and another in the vicinity of our present location.

We no longer rent or erect new buildings for new schools. We find it much more convenient to buy large houses with plenty of land and trees. They cost 50% less and allow us immediate possession. More important still is the fact that these buildings have been designed for family life. The stimulating effect of such a context, where everyone can feel at home and live and work as a large family in direct contact with nature is very positive.

We accepted the Ministry's proposition, in spite of our shortage of staff, because it was our great opportunity and the only possibility of extending our educational experience to all levels. Also, because this was the first official attempt made in this country to replace compulsory schooling with authentic education.

8 *A Summary of Thirty Years' Experience and Research*

This sudden and unexpected expansion of our activities put a great strain on our inner and outer resources until the first group of new teachers graduated in 1986. It became necessary to summarize everything we had learned in the course of the thirty years of intense practical research we had all shared. This chapter will be dedicated to this summary and divided into various subtitles. At first glance it may well seem that, in so doing, I am drifting away from my main theme: music. But it will soon become evident that just as research in music brought us inevitably into the field of education, so research in education brought us straight to the heart of music, its essential axis. "He who sings not, knows not how to live," says the ancient adage. This summary, in which music and education are so inextricably implicated, will also indicate what needs to be done and *why*; the *how* must necessarily be left to the creative capacity of all those concerned, teachers and pupils alike.

Research through practical experience requires faith in an intimate conviction. If this conviction is to be of any lasting value, it must be firmly rooted in an original idea, and thus respond to reality. In our cultured, civilized, occidental world, the reserve of original ideas has become dangerously depleted. Perhaps the area in which the lack of original ideas is most obvious is that of education.

Many years have passed since Whitehead denounced the fact that our scholastic systems are overburdened and paralyzed by inert, obsolete ideas which impede the appearance of any original ones. The general confusion as to what constitutes an original idea can be directly attributed to the type of schooling, materialistic upbringing, and mode of life to which we have all

59

been subjected from a very early age. Only too frequently, original ideas are confused with capricious personal inventions, aiming at novelty, which are both senseless and lacking in any permanent value.

An original idea is never new; it is as old as humanity. It reveals what is real, what is true. It can only vary in its form of representation. An original idea such as *"know thyself"* has echoed down the ages, from near and afar, losing none of its potency and validity. For original ideas are manifestation of that transcendent reality completely veiled by the illusory material world of appearances, but captured and transmitted by someone in a sudden instant of perceptive lucidity. It is a fleeting vision of totality which rises from the depths of what Jung has called "the collective unconscious," from our inborn, ontological wisdom with which we have lost touch. An original idea is never popular, because its vital logic is unquestionable, calling upon us to reconsider all our mental attitudes and the orientation of our lives.

When we opened our first school, thirty years ago, it was with the firm conviction that all children are born into this world as potential human beings with superabundant inner resources and creative power to enable them to grow up and mature in a normal way. Their task in this life and reason for existence is to become well-developed human beings, capable of projecting on their surroundings as "image of humanity." The essential mission of education would be to safeguard and stimulate this, their most natural evolution.

When people feel that things are going badly, they usually demand that they be changed, and in extreme causes will even start a revolution, generally involving bloodshed. But even a cursory glance at the history of humanity suffices to show that the fruits of such revolutions have usually perished quickly, their causes usually remaining untouched.

When we decided to attempt to do something in the field of education, things in that area were going from bad to worse, and the continual changes being effected were not even sufficient to hold in check the rapid deterioration of the situation. It was only through a prolonged and sustained practical investigation of the existing situation, working with young people, that we were eventually able to discover the root cause of the problem: a world population consisting mostly of under- or undeveloped human beings—in spite of their amazing scientific and technological achievements—owing to their lack of real education and the legal imposition of an annihilating system of schooling.

From the very beginning therefore, any attempt to change "things" was obviously futile and senseless. All that could and needed to be changed was the undeveloped human being that created and administered them—in the first instance, ourselves.

The central themes of our research have always been:

A) The original nature of infants, before distortion by the outer world

We find they have:

A natural capacity for perceiving everything and expressing themselves through gesture and image.

Spontaneity.

Innate wisdom.

Basic interior silence.

Active creativity.

An insatiable curiosity in exploring their surroundings and the possibilities of physical movement.

A vital logic, of a very different nature from adult reasoning.

A need to find the limits of their vital territory.

Desire to discover and do things for themselves.

Storytelling, singing, and dancing are a normal part of their lives.

If the matter is approached creatively, and no pressure is brought to bear, they learn to read and write at a very early age. This enables them to write, illustrate, and read the stories they tell.

The stories are mostly of mythical content.

Very young children make it abundantly evident that they are not ignorant, helpless individuals, needing an instructor to explain everything to them, and tell them what to do and how, but lucid, creative intelligences needing an authentic education to safeguard them from the distorting, paralyzing pressure of the adult world. Playing with them requires a great effort on our part to recover our own original nature in order to meet them on equal terms and not as deteriorated adults. It always perplexes them to discover that they see, do, and understand things we cannot.

B) The study of our present society, in which these infants will have to circulate, find a place for themselves, and live out their lives without succumbing to or being frustrated by its infirmities, its mode of life, and mercenary scale of values.

There can be little doubt, in the minds of intelligent people concerned or involved, that the most urgent, critical, and difficult problem now assailing humanity is that of education, since humanity's very survival is at stake. For many years now pupils, parents, and teachers alike have come to realize that the present system of compulsory schooling that we call education is illusory, anachronistic, and dangerously destructive of human values.

When the law was first imposed, schooling consisted mainly of learning to read and write, and to say a few prayers, all under a rigid, aggressive, and often brutal system of discipline and terror that survived well into this century. When, how, and why this arbitrary system came to be called education, would be a fascinating theme for a serious investigation. Be that as it may, the law continues to condemn all young children to enforced imprisonment within four walls, isolated from nature during the most delicate and decisive years of their lives, under the false pretext of educating them.

There is a general and insistent demand for educational reform, but you cannot reform something that does not exist.

To what disastrous extremes has this lack of education brought us? Every day the press, the TV, and the radio are full of references to them: violence, terrorism, murder, drug addiction, alcoholism, juvenile delinquency . . . to name a few. The number of delinquents far exceeds the capacity of our prisons, and the mentally ill that of our psychiatric services.

At this moment, humanity would seem to be whirling at an ever-increasing speed in the cesspool of life. A great number of the individuals comprising present-day society, instead of being able to contribute creative efforts to community life, can only discharge on it "the excrement of their minds." We, the adults, and those to whom we have delegated authority, are all responsible for what is affecting both us and the younger generations. We were all born happy, peace-loving human beings. But as a community, and in search of an illusory progress, we have chosen for ourselves a mode of life which impedes our natural evolution, and is leading us further and further away from our human condition.

The industrial revolution has had a great deal to do with this.

Enforced schooling has distorted life for us all, but the younger generations are no longer deceived by it. I well remember one of my Argentine grandsons, at the age of seven, asking me why his parents insisted on sending him to school. He had perceived and understood the implications of schooling immediately upon arrival."Why shut me up in a school where I sit for hours doing nothing and learning nothing? I learn much more in one day, playing, exploring, and fishing on the banks of a river, than I shall do in a year at school. Besides, if I stay at school, they will make an idiot of me."

Various generations have come and gone since the younger generations turned their backs on schooling and on the adult world and its mode of life; they want no part of it. They have closed their ears and their hearts to any attempt to persuade them, the new arrivals and healthy replenishments of the human race, to adapt and conform to a society which is seriously ill. They are no longer willing to listen to any one in authority, be it parent, teacher, or others. For many years now, the young people of our occidental world have been demanding the satisfaction of their basic needs and human rights. Their demands can be summed up in four words: Freedom, Love, Peace, Music.

Freedom	. . . to discover and fortify their individual identity, be themselves and realize their creative potentiality. . . . to remain firmly rooted in their first mythical-poetic world. . . . from the compulsion of authority and the devastating boredom of repetitive routine.
Love	. . . A need for real communication and immutable affection in their relationships with others.

Peace   . . . A desire to be free from the demands of competition and the endless, senseless conflicts assailing
them continually from within and without.

Music   . . . The reincorporation of natural spontaneous singing,
folk songs, and dancing and the playing of instru-
ments into their daily lives.

If ever we were offered an authentic and lasting basis for
real education, surely this was it. The lucidity of such wise
choices has always been a matter of amazement to me. They
made the right choices, but had no idea of the essential nature of
the things they demanded, and even less of how they could be
attained. They left their homes to establish themselves in small
communities where, for lack of experience and orientation, they
were quickly seized upon by innumerable sects, of diverse origins
and intentions. Thus the young people escaped from one prison
only to become entrapped in a worse one, which destroyed the
mental and physical health of the majority.

At this point it may be necessary to state that the "Hippie"
experiment, which became an important world phenomenon, has
no connection whatever, or any possible point of contact, with
our musical and educational research. Theirs was a gesture of
rebellion against all restraints; ours, a gesture of inner obedience
to the requirements of artistic expression. They made an attempt
to change the world and adjust it to their requirements in search
of self-satisfaction. They did, indeed, make a tremendous impact
on the world, but the results are far from being what they expected or hoped for. Our efforts are concentrated exclusively on
self-development; the transformation of ourselves into more
highly developed human beings.

Successive generations of young people continue to insist
on their demands, but their efforts are doomed to failure because
the homogeneous landscape of society offers them no point of
reference by which to orient themselves. Nor can they find, in
scholastic institutions, any opportunity of discovering, through
inner experience, the transcendent nature and quality of freedom,
love, peace, and music. Thus freedom has become caprice; love
has become identified with sex; and peace still implies a social
pact, based on mutual concessions.

Music has become widespread, indiscriminate emission of unmusical sounds which are both amorphous and reiterative. Song, which began by being spontaneous, poetic, folk, and imaginative is now hallucinatory, acting as a drug or a sexual stimulant.

Everyone is well aware of the alarming results of our present system of schooling, and the urgency of finding some solution. Yet the only proposals society has to offer seem to be higher salaries for teachers, longer hours of study and homework for pupils and an exigency of a higher level of efficiency in both, in order to make the final products saleable in an extremely competitive market.

Why are we so unwilling to admit that "like sheep we have gone astray" in the choice of or lifestyle and our education of the young, that we have abandoned the straight and narrow path of our human destiny to go chasing after a will o' the wisp, after the illusion we call progress, or a great future? The only great future looming on our horizon at the moment is total annihilation.

Let us look a little more closely at the effects of our present system of enforced schooling on young people. Presumably, we send them to school to learn to do certain things. No one can be compelled to learn. They will learn only if they are interested and willing. At present they are neither interested nor willing. They see no reason why they should be. Neither do they want to work for the sole purpose of earning money, as this signifies for them a lifetime's confinement under the pressure of authority and routine. They do not believe that this can be their only reason for existing.

Schooling offers them no opportunity to discover and develop their potential as human beings. They are violently and systematically uprooted from their first world, the world of myth and image. They are given no chance to bring into play their innate wisdom or their natural capacity for seeing that reality which lies beyond appearances. Their creative, imaginative, communicative, and affective channels are completely obstructed, the doors of their perception closed.

Thus do we convert healthy, lucid children, blessed with an inexhaustible store of innate wisdom, into paralyzed, stupefied, and totally disoriented adolescents, incapable of doing anything on their own initiative except destroy in the same measure as we have destroyed them. The senselessness and destruction of life, and not the joy of living, is the only lesson they learn, from bitter experience, under the present system of schooling.

One hears of many attempts, especially on the part of private enterprise, to provide education instead of schooling, but any successful ones are very hard to find, and even harder to sustain. People attempting anything of this nature have to swim against a very strong current of social prejudice, ignorance, fear, and stupidity. Any investment made is expected to make quick returns in terms of measurable results.

Education is a life-long process of self-discovery and evolution which cannot be measured. The word creativity has now become fashionable and is bandied from mouth to mouth with no idea of what it means, how it operates, or its profound significance. Another suggestion, ignored for many years, is now becoming popular: education through art. But we would be wise to ask those now proposing it what they know of education or art.

Governments all over the western world are now compelled to devote a large portion of their budgets, time, and concern trying to combat the social evils they themselves create by enforcing on the young a spiritually and mentally destructive system of schooling under the false nomenclature of education. What sense is there in continuing to create a social and individual situation that can only generate frustration, anxiety, violence, and despair?

Surely the obvious thing to do is to provide the young, from a very early age, with the real education they need. Today, medical, governmental, and other authorities are gravely concerned with creating immunity to disease, but no one seems to realize that by enforcing on children an annihilating system of schooling instead of providing them with education we leave them defenseless and impotent in the throes of a spiritual disease as lethal as any physical one. We transform them into "the walking dead."

C) Art as Education

The purpose of artistic experience is to keep open or reopen the doors of perception. It is only through these doors that the channels of creativity, communication, imagination, and affection can operate to connect us with our innermost selves and with reality. As the maximum intervention of all these channels is indispensable to education, it follows that artistic experience (not information) must be the axis of education. Within the various realms of artistic experience we have found that music, especially the singing of folk songs, is the quickest and most direct way to make contact with reality. Access to this experience must be immediate, free from all information, theories, and applied techniques; there is nothing to be taught, only experienced. We must sing to and for ourselves, not for listeners, straining our ears to detect the musical quality of the sounds we produce. It is impossible to make music with unmusical sounds. If we play an instrument, it must "sing" in the same way. Our musicality must not be limited to singing or playing an instrument; it must be in evidence when we speak, read, and move around.

The artistic experience of our students, at all levels, includes the singing of folk songs, folk dancing, the playing of instruments, painting, drawing, modelling, embroidery, tapestry, storytelling, the reading aloud, acting, and staffing of classical plays, a permanent contact with good poetry. This last permits them, at the age of 14-15, to take an English poem and produce its poetic equivalent in Spanish, with excellent results. English (and French) is learnt mainly through singing folk songs, reading aloud, and play acting. An important part of their education is that of making a creative contribution to the general community, sharing the vivifying experiences they enjoy with others. For example, they make periodic visits to a children's hospital to sing with the children and tell them stories—to the Institute for the blind, to sing with them, read interesting material and classical plays—and to other schools to sing and dance with the children and tell them stories or play act classical works.

D) The foundations of schooling

Schooling is inimical to education. An overview of the foundations of schooling can give us an inkling as to what is amiss. First of all, schooling is based on legal compulsion, which makes possible the indiscriminate imposition of models and methods by people who have no idea what education is about.

Schooling also is based on competition which sets everyone vying with their neighbor for supremacy. Hand in hand with competition comes a system of rewards and punishments which generate an atmosphere of fear and expectancy which in turn has a profound and lasting effect on the individual's attitude to life. Schooling is future-oriented, to which all things are relegated: happiness, employment and success. It exalts and makes into virtues duty, which is made into a civic virtue and the motive for action, and gratitude, where everyone must return reciprocally everything received and remain eternally indebted. Schooling isolates from nature, life and reality, presenting instead a fragmented universe in which we become observers and not participants. It stresses passive receptivity and immobility, where no creative activity is contemplated, only the repetition of other people's ideas. Book learning replaces experience, and theory supplants practice. Thereby the repetition of other people's ideas is placed above any artistic activity. Information is prized and memorized, and is valued more than real knowledge. This is enforced by an evaluation based on the false assumption that the students understand what they memorize. Evaluations and examinations dominate and determine the structure of schooling. They set up an authoritarian relationship between teachers and students.

Work and play are separated and set up as opposites. Time is for work, not for play. Time is money; play a waste. No time is allowed for meditation and daydreaming which are indispensable for all creative work. In such conditions, work, instead of being a creative stimulant, becomes drudgery, a daily sentence served in the hope of one day being able to play.

Finally, schooling, in its rigor and rigidity, with everything planned and foreseen, with everything rationalized, analyzed, and explained, treats children as ignorant and stupid, instead of lucid creative intelligences.

E) The foundations of education

These have not been placed in any specific order as they are all interdependent.

The present, here and now.

Reality, not ideals.

Faith in the invisible and intangible aspects of life and in one's own creative nature and potential.

Silence.

Peaceful, harmonious communal life. The singing, *a cappella*, of a Bach chorale can be a very enlightening experience for communal life as it should be led, if approached musically. Everyone first becomes familiar with all four voices, and then sings their own part quietly to and for themselves, with their maximum expressive capacity. Once you have heard a chorale sung in this way, you can never listen to it sung any other way.

Creative activities in all fields of human interest which are the different aspects of life.

Impersonal, ontological affection.

Play. All activities must have this quality, and be infused with the joy of living.

Knowledge and understanding, not information to be memorized.

Spontaneity, not merely the formalism of good manners.

Imagination. Perception and expression of sonorous and visual images.

Respect for the sanctity of life in all living creatures.

The daily creation of a sacred, uncontaminated space within which to live and play.

Direct contact with nature, and participation in its processes. We are a part of nature, not above it. We are part of the universe, too.

Lucidity, not cleverness.

Efficacy, not efficiency.

Originality.

Dialogue, not discussion.

Oral tradition. Myth, symbol, legend, and image.

No direction. Creative activities and internal growth must have freedom and cannot be directed.

Individuality, not personality.

Gesture and attitude, not action.

Inner growth and evolution. Educators and students alike are interested and engaged in the same task of growing up to be themselves, and thus are of mutual assistance.

Experience, not results.

No prizes.

No competition.

No models.

No examinations.

No memorizing

No repetition.

Single attitude towards everything and everybody.

Understanding and participation of parents.

Keeping open and unobstructed, or reopening creative channels through which reality can manifest itself and cosmic affection flow freely, to establish authentic and immutable communication.

All material used should be of the highest quality, not commercially invented for children.

No rigid division of time.

The perception of other human beings and all objects, always, as if for the first and only time.

Maintenance of our original equilibrium at the intersection of time and eternity.

Intensive experience in all forms of art, centered on music.

Musicality in song, speech, and movement.

Inner vision and hearing.

Seminal ideas instead of inert ones.

Incorporation of folk song into daily life as a proven traditional nourishment for the spirit, and of maximum educational value.

Immediate access to artistic experience, without the intervention of information and techniques.

Let no one be seduced by this list. These attractive qualities can only be achieved by inner conviction and a sustained effort. These are implacably real, extremely difficult to put into practice, and even more difficult to sustain, owing to the frailty of human nature with its inevitable ups and downs. This human instability produces profound periodic crises which have often threatened the continuation of the experiment. But so far, fortunately, we have been able to take them in our stride as growing pains. Faith, and intense work within and without, keep the ship afloat.

This experience could be summed up as an experiment born of an original idea, put into practice in daily life and oriented towards the full development of human beings. At most, at its best and at its worst, it is only a sincere attempt to implement our survival and fulfillment in a crazy world, an aspiration adhering to reality and stripped of illusions.

F) Our educational cycle

Public education for children should begin, at the latest, when they are three, whilst their original condition is still intact. Children should not commence their education later, because the most important work of the educational cycle, that of preserving and fortifying the original nature and integrity of the child, must be done between the ages of three and five.

A child's interest is in life in all its manifestation. Between the ages of three and five, children should be taken on a voyage for discovery through the macro and micro cosmos (through images) in order for them to realize that they are cosmic beings, understand how they came into being, and what their place and function is in this amazing universe. At this age, all this can be absorbed naturally by them with innocence and no malice.

By the age of five, most children have been totally uprooted from their first world and absorbed by the adult's world and mode of life. Particularly alarming instances are the amazing adult performances by very young children to be seen any day on TV, in commercials and regular programs for children and adults. Years ago, children were invited to show off their abilities within the family circle; now they are encouraged and applauded by the millions and paid high salaries. Neither the promoters, the parents, or the general public seem to have the vaguest notion of the gravity of this degree of corruption and exploitation, and so the law does nothing to protect the innocent victims. All parents would be very well advised to keep a careful watch over their gestures and attitudes with regard to their own and their children's lives.

All brothers and sisters should attend the same school, in order to receive the same education, thus avoiding conflicts amongst them at home and helping them to fuse home and school life.

Children should continue through, with no break, working with the same nucleus of educators, until they finish high school.

Our cycle here ends in a Teacher's Training Course (three years at undergraduate level) for those who wish to work as educators. This is most important, because unless sufficient educators are available, the present system of schooling cannot be replaced by education.

We admit a maximum of 25 pupils each year at the three-year-old level. These are then divided into smaller working groups. All groups, up to high school level, are in constant contact, and have some activities in common.At the 13-year-old stage, we complete this number (25) if there are any vacancies.

A serious problem arises at this stage because many parents, especially those who are professionals, who have paid no attention to their children's evolution, suddenly decide it's high time they got some serious schooling to prepare them for university and professional training; so they put an abrupt end to their education by removing them. The children's protests are of no avail. For this reason, there are always some vacancies at this stage.

With a group entering at the age of 13, the work to be done is that of recuperation, by intensive therapy. This is now extremely difficult because of their total rejection of the adult world, their distrust of any gesture of affection, and their disbelief in anything an adult proposes. We took on this work for the first time in 1984, and it took us nearly two years to penetrate this barrier and establish a healthy relationship.

To the final course for teachers, we admit 30 to allow for drop-outs. The first group graduated in 1986, and most of them continue to work with us. We had admitted 25 and twelve remained. The rest withdrew of their own accord. One graduate, with the collaboration of the third year students, has started a new school.

Education is necessarily an endless process which is not reversible. Education expands in a chain reaction, at its own pace. After 30 years, we now have hundreds of ex-pupils whose creative presence within society promotes the realization of human potentiality. They were scattered in the most varied of activities and professions. Some of them are working with us. Many are now parents bringing up their own children.

Once young people have spent fifteen or more years of their lives growing up in the right atmosphere to be themselves, mobilizing to the full their creative potentiality, and enjoying a daily participation in real life, they will never need any artificial stimulant to make them feel alive. The fun of real life is much more stimulating and fascinating than any substitute the market can offer them. Nor will they be interested in any of the hundreds of -isms that divide up humanity into warring factions on a permanent battlefield. Their own inner wisdom will be the compass with which to orient themselves for the rest of their lives.

Education must cultivate the profound religious sentiment with which we are all born but give no specific religious instruction, as this would bring it into the arena of sects and dogmas and fanaticisms, fount of bitter age-long conflicts and bloodshed. It is enough that an ever-present sense of the miraculous and sacred nature of the gift of life be maintained and respected.

G) The formation of future educators

These are not selected. Their preparation consists of a three-year course, at undergraduate level, during which they are submitted to an intense creative experience in all fields of art: music, folk-dancing, painting, drawing, theatre, literature (especially poetry), storytelling, etc., special emphasis being given to the development of their musicality in singing, speaking, reading and movement. The sole purpose of this experience is to help them rediscover and reopen the doors of their original perception, the channels of true affectivity, communication and creative expression, blocked by the exigencies of our materialistic society. The daily experience of self-discovery and self-recuperation is the only possible means of understanding what education is about and what their function as educators is to be. It must be maintained indefinitely after graduation. Three years' preparation barely suffices for students to achieve a basic orientation although during this time they assist other educators working with the youngest children. Some even find it impossible to free themselves from their habitual mental attitudes and prejudices, their inner insecurity offered them by a materialistic community. Only those who are sincerely convinced of the urgent necessity of changing their mental attitudes and mode of life can aspire to becoming educators.

No creative experience is possible unless there exists a propitious ambience of peace, inner silence, freedom, mutual respect, confidence, and affection. It is one of the educator's tasks to create this sacred uncontaminated space in which to live and play. Their task is not to instruct but to find and put into circulation authentic educational material with which to rouse the children's interest, curiosity, and imaginative and creative impulses. In this way educators and pupils unite to promote their normal growth to maturity and fulfillment as human beings.

H) The contribution of other investigators to the comprehension of music and education.

Into this warp of permanent musical-educational experience we had been weaving the multi-colored threads provided by those researching in the same or other fields: philosophy, history of religions, psychology, biology, philology, poetry, medicine, anthropology, and art. Of all available material we selected that which seemed to throw the strongest light on our own experience. These are listed in the appendix.

For us, each one of these investigators has made an important contribution to the deciphering of musical enigmas and their significance for education, but the results seem never to have been brought together before. As Angus Macintyre, a mathematician at Yale University, points out: "Problem solving inevitably involves new ideas, actually finding ideas that were not visible before. It's not just a question of going into something, breaking it up, and reconstructing it. It's not any simple process of analysis. It must necessarily involve some synthesis of ideas. You must bring together elements that were not brought together before." This is the main task I set myself in writing this book and the reason for the extensive quotations which now follow. A brief reference would not serve to connect them with each other, with music or education, especially as they deal more with gesture, attitude and experience than with action. They must be experienced to be understood. It was this interweaving of experiences that gradually brought to light the true nature of music and its relation to education. It reopened the horizon of music and education to the universe and recaptured their cosmic resonances.

In the course of a prolonged and varied musical-educational experience, we had observed many interesting phenomena, but we were always faced with the question of *how* and *why*. We all had the feeling that we were traversing a well-trodden road, that what we were searching for was nothing new but something that had been lost or forgotten; we were guided by our intuition. It was only in coming into contact with the experiences of investigators from other fields that we discovered what was operating to motivate these intuitions. These same studies, together with others cited here, gave us an insight into the existential significance of myth, symbol and image and why music and education depended on them for their existence.

The ideas of these research workers took us into a realm which can only be expressed in terms of myth, symbol, and image. The journey into the transcendental is the adventure of the mythical hero, who is for all of us, an exemplary model. For us it meant opening up our hearts and minds in order to be able to incorporate into our own musical and educational experience the cosmic experience of oneself to which these studies refer.

> If you came this way,
> Taking any route, starting from anywhere,
> At any time or at any season,
> It would always be the same: you would have to put off
> Sense and notion. You are not here to verify,
> Instruct yourself, or inform curiosity
> Or carry report. You are here to kneel
> Where prayer has been valid.

— T.S.Eliot *The Four Quartets*

9 *The Mythical Road to Reality*

It was Ariadne's thread which guided our footsteps through the many strange landscapes presented to us by the works of others, for as Joseph Campbell tells us,

> *The thread of flax she received from Daedalus, prototype of the artist-scientist, was harvested from the field of human imagination. Centuries of agriculture, decades of diligent selection, the work of many hands and brave hearts had contributed to the task of cutting, selecting and weaving this tightly twisted thread. Furthermore, we have now no need to set forth alone on this adventure, for the heroes of all times have preceded us. The labyrinth is known in all its details; all we have to do is follow the thread of the hero. And where we thought to find something abominable, we shall find a god; and where we expected to kill another, we shall kill ourselves. And where we thought to emerge from the labyrinth, we shall arrive at the very heart of our own existence, and there where we thought we should be alone, we shall be with all the world.*
>
> *Whether we listen with amused indifference to the fantastic sortilege of a red-eyed witch-doctor of the Congo, or read with refined fascination the pale translations of the mystic Lao-Tse, or try, time and time again, to break the hard shell of some argument of St. Thomas, or we suddenly capture the brilliant meaning of a strange Eskimo fairytale, we shall always find the same story, variable in its form, but nevertheless marvelously constant, and with an exciting and persistent suggestion that there is something more to be experienced than can ever be known or put into words.*

Man's myths have flourished in all the inhabited world, at all times, and in all circumstances. They have been the live inspiration of all that has arisen from the activity of man's body and mind. It would be no exaggeration to say that the myth is the secret entrance through which the inexhaustible energies of the universe flow into human cultural manifestations. Religions, philosophies, art, the social forms of traditional and historic man, the first scientific and technological discoveries, the visions which perturb our dreams, all emerge from the fundamental magic ring of the myth.

The amazing thing is that the characteristic efficacy which moves and inspires our profoundest creative centers resides in the simplest children's story, just as the taste of the ocean is contained in a drop of water, and all the mystery of life in the egg of a flea. For mythical symbols are not a fabrication; they cannot be ordered, invented or suppressed permanently. They are the spontaneous product of the psyche, and everyone carries within himself, intact, the germinal force of the fount.

But this kingdom, as psychoanalysis has shown us, is precisely the infantile unconscious. It is the realm into which we penetrate in dream. We carry it within us forever. All the ogres and secret helpers of our early infancy are there, vital potentials we have never been able to realize as adults; these and other parts of our being are there; because these seeds of gold never die. If only we could bring to light but a small portion of this lost treasure, we should experience a wonderful expansion of our powers, and we should grow to the stature of a tower. More than this: if only we could recover something forgotten not only by us but by our whole generation or by our whole civilization, we should be the donors of many gifts, and become the cultural heroes of the day.

And with reference to the hero's mythical journey he says:

The hero's first mission is to retire from the scene of the world of secondary effects to those causal zones of the psyche where the real difficulties reside. These the hero must clear up and eliminate, according to each particular case in order to reach an undistorted experience and assimilation of what C.G. Jung

*has called the 'archetypical images.' This process is known to
Hindu and Buddhist philosophy as 'viveka' i.e. 'discrimination.'*

*The archetypes that must be discovered and assimilated, are
precisely those which have inspired, throughout the annals of
human culture, the basic images of ritual, mythology and vision.
These 'eternal oneirical beings' must not be confused with the
symbolic figures personally modified which make their appearance in the nightmares or madness of the individual still in
torment. Dream is personalized myth, myth is impersonalized
dream. Both dream and myth are symbolic, as is the general
dynamism of the psyche. But in dreams the forms are distorted
by the peculiar difficulties of the dreamer, whilst in the myth,
the problems and the solutions shown are valid for all humanity.*

*The hero, therefore, is the man or woman who has been
capable of resisting and overcoming their personal and local
limitations and has achieved the general, normal and valid human forms. In this way their visions, ideas and inspirations
arise pristine from the primary fount of life and human thought;
thus their eloquence is not that of the present society and psyche
but of that inexhaustible fount in which humanity must be
reborn. The hero, as a modern man dies, but as eternal man . . .
perfect, non-specific, universal . . is reborn. His second mission
and achievement (as Toynbee declares and as all the mythologies
of mankind indicate) is to return to us transfigured, and teach
us the lessons learnt about the renovation of life.*

This had obviously been the unwitting orientation and
sense of the musical workshop.

The way out of the labyrinth is the way in, inwards to the
center, inwards to "the still point of the turning world," to "the
point of intersection of the timeless with time," towards the point
of origin from whence all human beings emerge from eternity
into chronological time. From the moment they are born, their
total well-being depends on their capacity to remain at this
crossroads, suspended in precarious equilibrium between the
temporal and eternity. It is easy to understand why the cross is
one of the most ancient of man's symbols.

To go inward towards the center is to enter the world of
myth. On approaching the world of myth, we discover that myth,

symbol and image operate simultaneously in an inseparable trinity. Our task is to explore this mythic poetical world in order to rediscover and reactualize our first world, the world of our infancy. The traditional man and the child become contemporaries.

> We shall not cease from exploration
> And the end of all our exploring
> Will be to arrive where we started
> And know the place for the first time.

—T.S. Eliot *The Four Quartets*

10 *The Sacred and the Profane*

At present, musical activity in the Occident is dominated by a sterilizing professionalism, and by a phenomenon known as popular music. This last, born of a healthy intuition, began by being amateur, a vitalization of folk creativity now rapidly disappearing from an urbanized world. Unfortunately it soon fell victim to the same merciless competition for the conquest of fame, prestige and money which characterizes the professional world, and most of its songs soon became stereotyped and void of all musical and poetic content. In both cases, music has become a commercially promoted article for consumption.

How came we to fall into such a state of vital and musical ignorance . . . that total ignorance I had experienced when faced with the enigmas of music, the strong current of ignorance in which not only musical activity, but the majority of human activities are today drifting.

If we are to take the real measure of this ignorance, it is useless to limit ourselves to studying its effects. Prehistoric man, according to Mircea Eliade, maintained that in order to understand things and know how to employ them, it was necessary to know their origin, how they came into existence. One must swim upstream, against the current, in order to reach the fount of origin. The effects we observe in the field of music have their causes, both immediate and remote, directly connected with the mode of life which man across the centuries has chosen for himself.

The different modes of life that man has created for himself and the resultant visions of the world would seem to be infinite; but on closer inspection, one thing that strikes us is the different quality of these visions. There is an old fable that runs:

"What a rare and exquisite flower," said the enthusiast.

81

"On the contrary," said the intelligent one. "It is only a thorny herbaceous plant of the genus Cardus, which in some parts of the country abounds like weeds."

"It is just a common thistle and not very nourishing," said the ass, swallowing it without further comment.

We owe to Mircea Eliade, in *The Sacred and the Profane*, the visionary prowess of having synthesized all the apparently different modes of life adopted by human beings across the centuries into two clearly defined categories: the *sacred* and the *profane*. In so doing, he is not making a moral evaluation but discriminating between the quality and orientation of two different modes of being.

Fortunately for us, Mircea Eliade, eminent historian of religions, has been able to rise above his erudition and pass on to us the vital sap he has extracted from it. This he achieves by taking another route, that of an inaudible dialogue and direct resonance expressed in essential Pentecostal language. The vital sap has given thousands of people a point of reference for their orientation in the homogeneous landscape of their daily lives. The mythical content of this quintessence communicates itself far beyond the actual words, through a profound ontological resonance to the sonorous flow of meaning.

I once had the opportunity of attending one of his lectures, here in Buenos Aires, in the Universidad Católica. The spacious hall was filled with people of all types, age and condition. He spoke in French, and I doubt whether, amongst those present, there were more than thirty people fluent enough in French to be able to follow a lecture of this nature. To obviate this problem, the organizers had placed at his disposal a university translator. But in spite of her excellent linguistic capacity, after a few minutes, the whole audience interrupted the lecturer to ask him not to use an interpreter as they could understand nothing. The interpreter withdrew and from then on no one had further difficulty in capturing the substance of what was being communicated. The translation had been correct but literal. When essential poetic language is translated literally it becomes meaningless and produces no resonances.

In a brief encounter with Eliade in the University of La Plata he asked me the nature of the work we were doing. I told him we were putting to the test in daily experience the two modes of being between which he had so clearly discriminated in *The Sacred and the Profane*. He laughed and said: "That book was written for people like you. It is only comprehensible through experience."

For Mircea Eliade, the *sacred* is the manifestation of something of an entirely different quality, of transcendental being, of reality. It manifests itself through myth, symbol and image. The *profane* is the material, homogeneous and illusory world of objects, persons and actions. The sudden appearance of the sacred in the homogeneous context of the profane world he defines as a *hierophany*. Any ordinary object such as a stone or a tree whilst retaining its nature as such, can become a *hierophany*. It all depends on the quality of our vision for, as the poet reminds us, "there are sermons in stones, books in running brooks." The irruption of the *sacred*, of something of a completely different nature and quality into a profane context, is a point of reference without which no orientation is possible. As we shall see later, this irruption of a *hierophany* into a profane homogeneous context is of vital importance for the comprehension of the nature of music.

He who chooses the sacred mode of being is the *homo religiosus*, which does not mean that he is associated with any sect or creed. Every human being is born as a *homo religiosus*, with an innate religious capacity and sentiment which is nourishment by essence. It is an essential part of his innate wisdom. The *homo religiosus* puts his whole attitude to life and his mode of being under the guidance of this inner wisdom.

Profane man is the *homo religiosus* who falls into a deep sleep, forgets his natural condition and even denies it, inventing for himself a desacralized world. His profane attitudes characterize his whole existence and deprive him of his former continuous connection with reality.

Testimonies abound and come from many different sources. I will quote one . . . a tale which the dervishes employ to keep their disciples awake. It is called *When the waters were changed*.

Once upon a time, Khidr, the teacher of Moses, called upon mankind with a warning. At a certain date, he said, all the water in the world which had not been specially hoarded, would disappear. It would then be renewed with different water, which would drive men mad.

Only one man listened to the meaning of this advice. He collected water and went to a secure place where he stored it, and waited for the water to change its character.

Upon the appointed date the streams stopped running, the wells went dry, and the man who had listened, seeing this happening, went to his retreat and drank his preserved water.

When he saw, from his place of security, the waterfalls again beginning to flow, the man descended among the other sons of men. He found that they were thinking and talking in an entirely different way from before; yet they had no memory of what had happened, nor of having been warned. When he tried to talk to them, he realized that they thought that he was mad; and they showed hostility or compassion, not understanding.

At first, he drank none of the new water, but went back to his place of concealment, to draw on his supplies everyday. Finally, however, he took the decision to drink the new water, because he could not bear the loneliness of living, behaving and thinking in a different way from everyone else. He drank the new water and became like the rest. Then he forgot all about his own store of special water, and his fellowmen began to look upon him as a madman who had miraculously been restored to sanity.

—Version of Idries Shah *Tales of the Dervishes*

It would be difficult to find a more eloquent image of the state of increasing madness now possessing humanity or of the real cause of it.

In any and every period of its existence, humanity has assumed one or other or both of these two modes of life, both individually and collectively. As a *homo religiosus* the individual is nourished by myths, symbols and images and is mindful to a greater or lesser degree of his reason for being and of innate wisdom. All he needs to feel a joyous and optimistic plentitude is the deep emotion he experiences on finding himself alive and creatively integrated into a live and generating universe . . . on feeling himself immersed in the strong current of cosmic affectivity which connects and nourishes all things created. In the words of Francis Thompson:

> *All things, by immortal power,*
> *near or far,*
> *hiddenly*
> *to each other linked are,*
> *that thou canst not stir a flower*
> *without troubling a star.*

But as a profane person, however, and for lack of this unique and permanent emotion, one finds oneself constrained to search avidly for new and short-lived emotions in a variety of personal experiences in order to feel alive, to allay an ever increasing state of boredom and to fill an affective, ontological void. To rouse oneself from slumber and a state of amnesia, realize one's situation and recuperate one's primitive state of *homo religiosus* demands of one an immense and unflagging effort, for one must undertake the alchemic task of transforming oneself and adequating one's whole life to an attempt to unveil the greatest mystery of all: one-One.

This naturally requires imagination, that is to say, the capacity to apprehend and vibrate in unison with the poetic mythical language of imagery. "To have imagination," says Eliade, "is to have the benefit of the inner treasure of a continuous and spontaneous flow of images. But here spontaneity does not mean arbitrary invention, but the reactualization of exemplary creative gestures. To have imagination is to be able to see the world as a whole; and the function and power of the images is to make manifest all that cannot be expressed in concepts. For this reason, the misfortunes and ruin of the man who lacks imagination is that he finds himself totally disconnected from the most profound reality of life and from his own soul."

11 *The Two Modes of Life and Their Implications*

The sacred and profane attitudes which characterize the two modes of being, affect all the planes and aspects of one's life. Both attitudes have serious implications into which we must now look more closely, for it is these attitudes which in the last instance determine whether, in spite of apparent musical ability, one is a musician or not. Each mode of life has its own language and mode of expression.

Mircea Eliade observes that a totally profane world, a completely desacralized cosmos, is a recent discovery of the spirit of man. Modern man has desacralized his world and assumed a profane existence. This desacralization characterizes the total experience of non-religious persons in modern societies; for this reason they find it increasingly difficult to understand the existential dimensions of the *homo religiosus* of archaic societies, and of the one that exists within them. When speaking of the *homo religiosus* and of profane man, we are referring to the same individual and his two possible modes of being in the world, his two possible orientations.

As *homo religiosus* all his gestures and attitudes obey transcendental exemplary models conveyed to him by the myths; all his acts are of a ritual nature: the building of a house, the way of inhabiting it, the fabrication of utensils, food, eating, the cultivation of alimentary plants, sex, work, the treatment and curing of illnesses, etc. He knows himself to be a cosmic man; ontologically, he feels that in this cosmos he has his allotted place, function and meaning.

It is for this reason that he assumes the enormous responsibility of collaborating creatively with the life of the Cosmos by creating his own world and procuring the survival of plants and animals. He is neither the origin nor the end of anything, but simply a well-tuned instrument through which everything can be realized sacramentally as a work of Grace.

As profane man his gestures and attitudes lack exemplary models and are therefore senseless. For the same reason, his acts are personal, capricious, utilitarian. They lack grace and rituality. He acts as a terrestrian, totally disconnected from the cosmos for which he neither feels nor assumes any responsibility, since within it he finds no place, function or reason for his existence. At most he will perhaps assume the moral, social and historic responsibilities that society demands of him. His profound sense of ontological insecurity creates in him a feeling of anguish and anxiety that drives him to procure for himself an illusory material security. As a consequence, everything exists to be used and exploited. He creates for himself a world in which everything can be bought and sold, and in which he himself becomes one more saleable object on the market. Everything begins and ends with him.

The difference of quality between these two antagonistic but not contradictory worlds, sacred and profane, is so great, that in order to comprehend it, it is necessary to experience it continually in everyday life. With the idea of facilitating this task for my students, I made, with their assistance, a draft of a map of the two terrains, inviting them to amplify or modify it for themselves. It was a very rewarding experience. One must take into account one's interests and desires and find out to which world they belong. I include this first draft because it may interest my readers to try the experiment for themselves, by adding or suppressing elements. All the component elements of both worlds are present in each of us. We are not sacred *or* profane, but sacred *and* profane, since we belong both to time and eternity. The profane world is that which one inhabits at a psychological level, where we are swayed by circumstances, contingencies, emotions, fears, ambitions, and continually besieged by memories, projects and illusions. In the sacred world one lives on the level of being, with an ontological anchorage in the immutable being which is not contingent.

The constituent elements of these two worlds are coherent, nontransferable and mutually implicated. Putting them to the test in daily life one discovers for instance that liberty and spontaneity both belong to the sacred world and that the one implies the other and both are the fruit of a strict inner obedience.

Perhaps we could represent these two spheres thus:

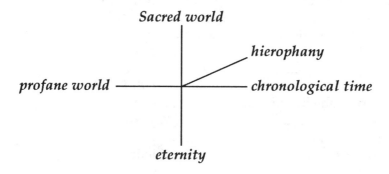

Sacred world	Profane world
being	person
wisdom	knowledge
mind	intellect
percept	concept
revelation	deduction
formation	information
integration	differentiation
meanings	words
symbolic Pentecostal language	literal language
live communication	rhetoric, discourse
ontologic	psychologic
creation	invention
anonymity	prominent figure
universal	personal
mobile	fixed
rite	spectacle
hear	listen
amazement	surprise
presence	absence
infinite	finite
reality	illusions, appearances
love	to be in love, love-sickness
principles	laws

Sacred world	*Profane world*
ineffable	explicable
pure intelligible emotion	amorphous emotivity
consciousness	conscience
sense	absurdity
coparticipation	competition
quality	quantity
image	object
imaginative	hallucinatory
internal obedience	caprice
humility	pride
dispossession	possession
spontaneity	habit
eternity	chronological time
reason	reasoning
feeling	thought
comprehension	understanding
imagination	reflection
experience	theory
genesis	accumulation
verb	noun
poetic	prosaic
dialogue	prattle, conversation
myth	logic
individuality	personality
originality	novelty
open	closed
apprehension	learning
see	look
participant	spectator
eternal present	past, future
intemporal	temporal
permanent	fugacious
original, adequate and unforeseeable *techne*	learnt techniques for general application
spontaneous gesture	conventional gesture, style, fashion
truth	opinions
self-evident	demonstrable

Sacred world	Profane world
vital lucidity	vital stupidity
intelligence	cleverness
self-creation	self-affirmation
expression	technical demonstration
efficacy	efficiency
symbol	sign
security	insecurity
faith	distrust, fear
surrender	conquest
liberation	imprisonment
freedom	slavery

The perfect place for a human being is at the crossroads, which is its primordial position. At the crossroads, with one foot in time and the other in eternity, one is in a position to act as a channel of Reality and become a *hierophany*. This term is employed by Mircea Eliade to signify the appearance and manifestation of reality, of the sacred, of something completely different not pertaining to our profane world, in objects and beings belonging to the sphere of the profane.

If we now refer these two possible modes of existence to musical experience, we shall discover that all the requisite elements pertaining to the making of real music are to be found in the sacred world. The making of real music involves imagination, creation, inner obedience, faith, spontaneity, affectivity, freedom from prejudice and eternal restraint, originality, genesis, participation, anonymity and total surrender. The musician must be able to cross the threshold of chronological time into an eternal present in order to create a rhythmic flow of significant sound images of which he is not the author but the transmitter. He must let the music play him and not the reverse.

This may sound as though I'm saying that to make real music one must be a perfect human being. Nothing could be further from the point I am making. On the contrary, the capacity to make music is inborn in all of us, and is the quickest and most direct means of making contact with the center, with reality. It is simply a question of orientation, of adopting the right attitude. The correct attitude will bring into play all the necessary requirements for obtaining what is desired. Things pertaining to one attitude are not interchangeable with those of the other. If you want to see the sun rise you must look to the east; it's no use looking to the west.

The creation of real music, then, is not merely a question of making sounds, of playing or singing the notes, but the establishment of an attitude which will allow a live rhythmic flow of sound images. These images channel a symbolic mythical content which orients us towards a sacred reality by turning our attention inwards. This, naturally, involves our inquiring into the nature of myth.

12 *Myth*

In a profane materialistic world, myth, symbol and image lose all their multivalidity and their power of educating and orientating, for the intellect makes a literal reading of them, depriving them of content and meaning. Myth, symbol and image operate simultaneously to make us vibrate in resonance with a manifest reality.

The myth is a creation of the human spirit. Assailed in their temporal persons by the contingencies of life, human beings seek a timeless anchorage for their being. The myth relates sacred immutable realities, how all creation came into existence at the beginning in a sacred primordial time. Mircea Eliade says that "the sacred is the Real. Nothing pertaining to the sphere of the profane participates in Being, since the profane is not ontologically founded on myth and lacks exemplary models. All that the myths tell us about the creative activity of the gods, belongs to the sphere of the sacred and therefore participates in Being. On the contrary, everything one does on one's own initiative without a mythic model belongs to the sphere of the profane; one's activity is therefore vain, illusory and aberrant. The more religious one is, the greater is the number of exemplary models one has at one's disposal for the guidance of one's actions and behavior. Or rather, the more religious one is, the more one inserts oneself into Reality and the less risk one runs of losing oneself in actions which are non-exemplary, subjective and finally aberrant."

Whilst the profane world denies all validity to myth, branding it as unreal and noxious for the education of the young, reality makes manifest its magisterial function: to provide us with exemplary models for all the basic aspects of human life . . . food, work, education, sexuality, etc. Eliade points out that "one cannot become a real human being unless one adopts the teachings of the myths and imitates the gods."

Georges Gusdorf reveals for us other aspects of the nature, function and *modus operandi* of the myth. He says that: "The myth structures our first world and is intimately connected with the first apprehension that a human being has of himself and his surroundings. With the aid of his mythic consciousness, traditional man achieves a single perception of his vital horizon (unlike us who have two: subjective and objective). For him the myth was not a myth, but Truth itself.

"The myth is an ontological structure that perpetuates a reality, and is felt and experienced before its intelligibility and formulation. It affirms the totality, the radical identity of an ontological unity. The maintenance of existence demands the pursuit of a fragile, menaced equilibrium, the smallest rupture of which imposes severe penalties . . . ontological insecurity, which creates anxiety. The myth affirms itself as a means of returning to order.

"Rediscovered in its vital context, the myth manifests itself as the spontaneous mode of life; not as a theory or doctrine, but as the apprehension of things and beings and of oneself, of behavior and attitudes,as the insertion of human beings into reality. It is in the mythical landscape that one comes to understand oneself. It is there we play our part. The mythical consciousness orients a human being's actions with reference to a horizon defined once and for all. The rite reactualizes the myth. The rite is the myth in action. The primitive ontology is an ontology put into action spontaneously by the totality of the individuals.

"The ontological region discovered by the myth is inaccessible to the experience of superficial logic. The commencement of learning coincides with an uprooting from existence." The myth of Adam and Eve as it appears in Genesis in the Jewish-Christian Bible, bears witness to this. The first pair lived immersed in Being and was nourished by the Presence. By eating of the tree of knowledge, they exiled themselves from Paradise, from the sacred world, condemning themselves to earn their sustenance by the sweat of their brow. They had exchanged the comprehension of a participant for the knowledge of an observer.

13 *Communal Health and Sickness*

What we now call culture and civilization, by invading traditional communities, put an end to their original gestures and their primordial spontaneous mode of life. This polar change of direction that inverted the vital scale of values has not been innocuous. It has turned a healthy community into one that is seriously ill, and what is even more alarming is that this society suffers from a kind of vital amnesia which prevents it finding its way back to health. This illness is no longer the exclusive fate of some contemporary archaic peoples. We, the invaders from the civilized world, had already been invaded by the same disease, which has now reached worldwide proportions, namely ontological disconnection from reality and from the mythical landscape of our existence, arising from erroneous attitudes to life, the root cause of stress and anxiety. W. H. Hudson in *The Purple Land* bears witness to this: "Ah yes, we are all vainly seeking after happiness in the wrong way. It was with us once and ours, but we despised it, for it was only the old common happiness which Nature gives to all her children, and we went away from it in search of another grander kind of happiness which some dreamer assured us we should find. We had only to conquer Nature, find out her secrets, make her our obedient slave, then the Earth would be Eden, and every man Adam and every women Eve. We are still marching bravely on, conquering Nature, but how weary and sad we are getting! The old joy in life and gaiety of heart have vanished."

We have only to walk along a crowded street or through a railroad terminus at rush hour to realize how real this image of a sad, tired humanity is. Why this sadness; why this tiredness? Was this a natural inevitable condition, inherent in human nature or was it the result of an acquired mode of existence and attitude to life? Was this the result centuries of culture and civilization had produced? Our own experience had shown us that music could lift us momentarily out of the stresses and strains of everyday life, out of weariness, dissatisfaction and anxiety into a world of well-being, plentitude and joy of life. It could restore us to health. What we did not know was why and how. It was with the aid of the findings of investigators in other fields which shed new light on our experiences that we were able to discover the causes producing effects. For this reason, I am quoting them here as material having a direct bearing on the elucidation of our own findings. Thus we came to realize that for music to produce in us such an effective transformation, all that was needed was a change of attitude; we had to turn our attention inwards towards our innermost self and allow the music to reincorporate us into the mythical landscape of our first world and immerse us in impersonal cosmic affectivity.

During the 1960s in the western world, there was a sustained effort on the part of the younger generations, voicing their total disagreement with the establishment, to return to the basic meaningful elements of life. One of these elements, perhaps the most crucial, was certainly music, intimately linked to their desire for peace, freedom and love. They failed in their attempt because of a lack of orientation. They were asking for the right things, but had no idea how to obtain them.

Within the establishment, musical therapy for the treatment of a sick humanity became a widespread practice. This was based, I think, on a false assumption, for music is not a therapy but a ritual experience of rebirth. As Mircea Eliade observes, "life cannot be mended only regenerated." I have found that in practice, the musicians and doctors working together in this field are ignorant of the real nature of music and its *modus operandi*.

The widespread conviction of the general public, acquired through experience and the faint stirrings of an innate wisdom, that music is a basic necessity affecting health, has given rise to functional music, often of questionable musical content, and to the extraordinary technical advances in the production of audio equipment.

Now it is a very common sight to see people walking the streets with headphones clapped to their ears, listening to radio or cassettes, and students at all levels studying in the same way. When deprived of this equipment, many become seriously perturbed. Somehow people feel that listening continuously to music (although what they listen to is a crucial problem) in some way helps them to preserve their sanity whilst living in a maddening, senseless world. Unfortunately, the general public and, for that matter, many professional musicians are unable to discriminate between the musical (which transmits mythical content through symbol and sound image and thus connects us to reality) and the unmusical. The unmusical is not innocuous, for it foments illness, not health.

With reference to this, Georges Gusdorf remarks: "The brutal disappearance of the regime of mythic consciousness on coming into contact with Europeans has reduced traditional peoples to a kind of poverty and misery both physiological and spiritual. This is the reason for their mass mortality to which statistics bear terrifying witness.

"What would appear to manifest itself is the extinction of the desire to live. It would seem as if the native found himself less resistant to pathogenic agents and the ordinary difficulties of life. He succumbs because he finds himself unadapted. He becomes prematurely aged, fatigued and weak, brutally detached from all that bound him to the ritual landscape of his existence. From now on he has lost his allotted place on earth and his agony is part of the objective agony of mythic reality. He languishes because his very reason for existing has disappeared for ever.

"Nothing could bear truer witness to the existential significance of ontology. It is not just a play of words or ideas but a matter of life and death. One's transcendental cipher is the foundation of one's being in the world. The loss of one's ontological place, guaranteed by the myth and destroyed by reflection, is felt as a transgression, a source of insecurity and anxiety. The myth signified participation and implication. The reflexive conscience substitutes for this regime of confusion a new system of separation and opposition.

"Logic and myth are at two distinct levels; they are not two interchangeable ciphers of interpretation existing on the same level. Mythic consciousness is an inalienable structure of human beings. It carries with it the first sense of existence and of its original orientations."

A second testimony comes from Dr. James Halliday, from his study of a sick society in his book *Psychosocial Medicine.*

"Owing to a lack of opportunity for participating creatively in the flow of life and thus procuring their psychological development and maturity, human beings are unable to gain access to that hidden source of energy that sustains life in order to establish and regenerate themselves permanently in that which *is* . . . and consequently become psychologically ill." Modern methods of propaganda and publicity exploit this circumstance, thus making matters worse. "At this moment, the human species is in exactly the same trance as so many others on the point of extinction.

"To realize that we are living in a sick community whose social infirmity is the reflection of our own psychological disorders, with their erroneous emotional and intellectual attitudes, is most disquieting. But more disquieting still, is to know that this social illness implies a profound biological process which tends towards a progressive devitalization and sterilization, which can lead to genetic extinction. And within the limits of our present knowledge, we have no idea whether the present biological trend is reversible or not.

"What we do know is that only in so far as we can convince human beings to face up seriously to the problem of a sick community (which exists within and outside ourselves) does there exist any possibility of rescuing man from slipping back into chaos and genetic extinction (whether gradual as in the case of increasing sterility, or sudden as in the case of an atomic war) and reorient him towards health, towards the constitution of a healthy society whose members would be united by bonds of affection and a common creative purpose."

The great European myth of Parsifal and the Sinful King, cited by Eliade in *Images and Symbols*, is another testimony, equally real and eloquent, to the present state of health of our society, and its cause.

"Everyone knows of the mysterious illness that had paralyzed the old king who possessed the secret of the Holy Grail. But he was not the only one to suffer; everything around him fell into ruins, became sterile; the palace, the towers, the gardens; the animals no longer increased and multiplied, the trees bore no fruit, the fountains ran dry.

"Many doctors had tried to cure the Sinful King, but in vain. Day and night he was visited by nobles who all began by asking after the king's health. Only one visitor—poor, unknown and even a little ridiculous—permitted himself to ignore etiquette and courtesy. His name was Parsifal. Ignoring courtly ceremonial, he went straight up to the king, and without preamble asked him: 'Where is the Holy Grail?'

"At that very instant, everything was transformed. The king rose from his sickbed, the rivers and fountains began to flow anew, the vegetation was reborn, the castle was miraculously restored. Parsifal's words had been sufficient to regenerate the whole of nature. But in these few words lay the whole problem, the only problem of interest, not only to the king, but to the whole cosmos: 'Where is the real, the sacred, the center of life and the fount of immortality? Where is the Holy Grail?' To no one had it occurred to ask this central question until Parsifal posed it, and the world was perishing on account of this religious and metaphysical indifference, and because of such a complete lack of imagination and desire for the Real."

14   *The Nature of Sound*

In order to discover the original nature of music and musicians, we must follow the example of the sinful king and return to the center in order to become contemporary with the creation of the world. We must return to our first mythic, poetic and ineffable world in which myth, symbol and image operate simultaneously to bring us into the presence of reality. We can only perceive and understand this reality by vibrating in resonance with it, by experiencing it, not by intellectual cogitation. It is all important for a musician, whose only working material is sound, to comprehend the essential nature of this material . . . his relationship to it and how and why he is affected by it. Every sound we produce affects not only us but everything around us—why?

Let us approach this world of sound with the aid of a synthesis of megalithic myths of the Creation made by Marius Schneider in *El espíritu de la música como origen del símbolo*. These myths project in us powerful images which contain no information but only an ancient wisdom which reorientates us towards the center. We must surrender ourselves to them with faith and confidence in order to be able to "walk on the waters" . . . the only way to accede to manifest reality and cross the threshold between the sacred and the profane. In the words of Gaston Bachelard, "these images resound in the depths of our being without disturbing the surface," leaving us in the presence of a manifest and inexplicable reality.

Marius Schneider observes that "the significance of the potency of sound as a fundamental, autonomous and acoustic substance and as a profound stratum of man's dream world is universally described, above all, in the cosmographies, the rites

and philosophies of dreams (Traumphilosophien) of megalithic
cultures.

"An essential feature of their myths of the Creation is that
the universe always emerges from the immaterial."

Another common trait of many myths of the Creation is
that this new world which emerges from the immaterial comes
out of primordial silence and darkness.

Marius Schneider continues: "In the beginning there is the
mute desire of the Supreme Spirit to create the world. To this end,
the Spirit first causes the vacant cosmic space to emerge from his
breath, whilst dreaming of the primary models of the world in the
form of inaudible and inconceivable syllables. This takes place in
utter darkness in the extreme North. The Supreme Spirit then
exhales an inaudible song of praise, out of which emerges the
body of the Creator of the world, who must translate the original
sound into a new dream existence, independent of the Supreme
Spirit or Essence.

"Once the creator serenely, and devoid of all passion, in
the first dawn of the Orient, made audible the inaudible desire of
the Supreme spirit, this grew and expanded like a singing tree, or
like a cloud of humid sonorities, within vacant space, filling it
with sound. With this, the creator concludes the first phase of
Creation, purely acoustic."

Here we can observe another common trait of these early
myths of the creation. The first thing to emerge from primordial
silence and darkness is a sound energy, capable of creating or
destroying form, whose high frequency makes it inaudible.

"When the creator (who was probably the singing primeval sun) moved towards the East, his sonorous, delicately ethereal
songs gradually became luminous. This brings us to the second
period of Creation in which the primeval dreamt-of sounds made
themselves visible. These subtly sonorous images were the
'names' of the gods and of all future creatures." (In the archetypical memory of humanity, there still persists even today the notion
that to name is to create. We also show a vague atavistic memory
of original silence and darkness when we put out the lights and
remain silent before beginning a concert or a play at the theatre.)

"The first things to be created therefore, were names and
intelligible sounds which, under the luminous rhythms of the

sun, had liberated themselves from the nebulous mass of primeval sounds and were situated between the original void, or nothingness, and the posterior concrete object pertaining to its name. They were the words or songs through which the creator had sonorously formulated the desire of the Supreme Spirit. This sound was the original substance which, like an infinite resonator, filled vacant cosmic space.

"But the creatures who had become visible, then desired for themselves a concrete body and corporal weight. This they achieved in the third phase of the Creation by precipitating themselves, with their singing luminous rhythms, into amorphous matter, thus imposing on it the imprint of form and meaning. In this way the planets, the moon and the earth were born, and finally plants and the inhabitants of the world. This brings to an end the dream phase of infancy of the universe (Traumzeit).

"In the beginning there was inaudible, invisible sound, which later became audible, visible and resplendent. Finally the sound images transform themselves into the concrete objects which correspond to their names. This they achieved by precipitating themselves into formless matter.

"The fundamental structure (ethereally sonorous, spiritual, active and celestial) was first obscure, then resplendent and finally visible. On the contrary, the material world which later emerged was passive, sluggish, dissonant or mute. But as the first friction between these two antagonistic worlds took place during the third period of Creation, an intermediate world was born, that is to say, the first material substance in which, however, the spontaneously vibrating Spirit imposed vibration on mute matter in such a way that it became as resonant as a musical instrument.

"This intermediate semi-concrete world came into being because the ethereal, originally sonorous Spirit submerged itself into matter, shaping it at will, thus creating a world in which the potency, till then ethereally sonorous, suddenly became audible in matter. Naturally, this was on account of the Spirit having created for itself an abode or channel capable of vibration, with the aid of which it could manifest itself freely.

"It is very noteworthy that this elemental significance of the acoustic phenomenon should have been constantly omitted in the investigation of symbols, in spite of the fact that ancient literature and ethnographic findings abound in proofs establishing the voice as the supreme manifestation of creative power, and the most acute form of potency."

15 *Daedalus, Archetype*

These old myths tell us how an original sound energy operated to create an energetic cosmos capable of transmuting itself at a given moment into a material world. In this they parallel the modern scientific investigations of Maxwell, Einstein, Brogli, Jeans, Planck, Bohr, Schrödinger, Eddington and many others.

How could megalithic people create these myths as presented by Schneider except through the experience of singing?

Prehistoric man was an artist-scientist, a creative *homo religiosus,* who by experiencing the forces operating in the universe, came into play with them in an attempt to assure and understand his existence. This artist-scientist of whom Daedalus was the exemplary model, operated from an invisible, intangible and ineffable world. The investigators were initiates who assumed the creative gestures of the gods. In more modern times, the original unity of art and science disintegrated into two opposite fields of interest and activity, two distinct attitudes . . . a criterion which still holds.

Science modified its creative attitude and began to operate from the visible, tangible world of the senses, the world of effects not causes. It began to make an objective reading of the landscape, owing to the change of attitude of the investigators involved. Only the alchemists and the creative scientists continued to maintain an intimate relation between their attitude to life and their activity.

With a causalistic, mechanical criterion, science now expressed its vision of the world in concepts, employing classical logic. Consequently, the essential relationships which connect and infuse meaning into all the elements of the universe became

105

invisible for them. Observed with this materialistic criterion, we appear on the landscape as objects of flesh and bone. For this science, all that could not be observed and named did not exist.

It is most interesting to see by what strange paths and employing its own techniques, especially during the last hundred years, scientific research, with no such intention, has found itself obliged to change its course and steer in its original direction, for, penetrating into subatomic and supragalactic worlds, concepts for the expression of its findings lost validity and efficacy and had to be replaced by symbols. In the light of present-day investigations, our solid matter of flesh and bone has gradually dissolved, transforming itself anew into precarious nuclei of concentrated energy, subject to the dynamic organization of a universal cosmic energy.

The original artist-scientists were cosmic beings. As such, they participated in the dynamism of cosmic energy. Later scientists changed their mode of life and became merely observers. The causes remained occult.

But now modern research workers have been compelled to include themselves in their investigations. Having now returned to the world of symbol and reality, their only chance of penetrating further into the mystery of life is as participants, assuming once again, we hope, the responsibility of collaborating in the maintenance of cosmic life. In this resides, in great part, humanity's hope of survival.

Science now has to work with symbols in order to apprehend that other reality which underlies the world of the senses and discover the significant connections which organize it. The modern scientist has to act once more as the artist-scientist he was originally, like the mythic Daedalus.

> *Behind the sensual world, we are compelled to accept a second world: the real world.*
>
> — Max Planck

> *We belong to the world of dimension, but come from the non-dimensional. Close the first and open the second.*
>
> — Jalalt uddin-Rumi

*The intellect is characterized by a natural inability to compre-
hend life.*

— Bergson

Jean Wahl, in his *Introduction to Philosophy,* remarks: "We
have now come to a point where on the one hand, scientific
development has shown, in all its aspects, the inadequacy of the
old schemes of space, time and causality, and on the other hand
the development of Gestalt psychology and psychoanalysis with
its idea of superdetermination, have combined to make us understand the necessity for finding new ways of thinking. The classical
principles have dissolved into thin air; structures have exploded
into a thousand pieces, and even the very things these structures
contained have disappeared. We now find ourselves confronted
with a jungle of phenomena of which classic philosophies give us
no idea. We are in a no man's land, and what is more, a territory
for which we have no words. In the discovery of these new
kingdoms of thought, certain poets and painters can be of great
help to us." Why exclude musicians?

More than a new way of thinking, what we really need is
to reactualize symbolic thought, the natural language of our first
world and of traditional man. "Verily I say unto you, except ye be
converted, and become as little children, ye shall not enter into
the kingdom of heaven." (St. Matthew, XVIII, 2).

Let us recall the testimony of Gusdorf: "Mythic consciousness orients human action with relation to a horizon defined once
and for all time. The rite reactualizes the myth. The rite is the myth
in action. Traditional ontology is an ontology set in motion spontaneously by the totality of individuals, with a creative gesture."

A musician, born and trained in a modern, industrialized,
materialistic society, must therefore consider what attitude and
what gestures are compatible with the making of real music. His
habitual conceptual, possessive and utilitarian attitudes will be of
no help to him here, for he must impose nothing personal on the
music but surrender himself completely to the dictates of expression which arise from a strict inner obedience.

Real music is not the product of personal psychological,
emotive activity. On the contrary, it is a manifestation of immu-

table Being with which the musician must be ontologically at one. He must participate; he must *be* the music. He must allow the music to play *him*.

We have seen that the attitude and gestures of traditional communities, which are also those of our first world, are those which a musician must recapture and reactualize if he would cross the threshold of music.

16 *St. Bernard*

If the material with which a musician works is sound, it naturally follows that the decisive element for his activity is his ear; not only his hearing, but that of inner discernment between musical and unmusical sound. As this is something which is often overlooked or underrated, we must look more closely into the question of hearing.

Let us return for a moment to the megalithic myths as presented by Schneider, for it is these myths, in action, that will eventually give us the clues to all the enigmas that surround music and the musician.

It tells us that the Creation was sonorous and in it, the ear held preeminence over the eye. First came sound, then light. In virtue of the creative activity of an original sound energy, all creatures came into existence.

Many myths emphasize the preeminence of the ear over the eye. In the profane material world, the eye has substituted for the ear. In this matter it is interesting to observe and take into account the attempt that St. Bernard made to restore to the ear its original and legitimate priority over the eye.

St. Bernard of Clairvaux (1090-1153) gave his monks specific instructions for the building of the Cistercian Abbeys of his time. They had to be authentic oratories for the reception of the Divine Word by the inner ear. To this end they had to be built on a human scale, determined by the normal reach of voice and ear. They should be rectilineal (curves were permitted only in the vault, so that the resonances might acquire an ethereal quality). They must be built of bare stone with no irregularities in its surfaces which might distort the resonances. They should be devoid of furniture and all hangings that would mute and absorb sound, and of all adornments, paintings and vitraux that would distract the attention of the inner ear to the outer eye to the detriment of the Word of God. The apertures should be few and small, in order to create a propitious atmosphere of silence and penumbra. Hubert Larcher in his study of the Cistercian Abbeys says: "The stone vibrates with the choir, the temple is an immense musical instrument, the rhythm of whose song is created by man's breath. For this instrument to be perfect as a whole as well as in its parts, it should take as a model the unity of the cosmos. It must obey the laws of the universe on a human scale. The house of God, which is also that of man, should be erected as a mesocosmos between the micro and macrocosmos, thanks to the orientation of the stone and divine proportion."

Why did St. Bernard impose such drastic, specific conditions? Evidently, as many other visionaries across the centuries, he was drawing attention and trying to avoid the serious danger which menaced humanity if they allowed the eye to usurp the legitimate priority of the ear . . . a danger as lethal for the spirit as the atomic bomb for the body, all the more so because it passes unnoticed, it remains occult. St. Bernard says that "in matters of faith, and to know the truth, the ear is superior to the eye. Entering through the ear, Evil has clouded vision. By the same route, if we open the ear, the Verbal Remedy can regenerate it. For you must know that the Holy Ghost, in order to promote spiritual development, uses the same method. It educates the ear before entertaining the eye. Why do you insist on seeing? What you should do is awaken the ear. The ear will restitute the eye if our attention is pious, faithful and vigilant. Only the ear has access to the Truth, because it perceives the Verb. One must awaken the ear and exercise it in order to receive the Truth."

It would seem unnecessary to stress the importance of the ear in musical activity and experience. Nevertheless in practice it has been neglected and in many cases substituted for by the eye. As far as audition is concerned, musical audition and acoustical audition are two different things, involving the inner and the outer ear.

The basic problems from which our twentieth century society suffers are simply the concretion of the dangers that St. Bernard denounced and tried to avoid. In order to understand more fully the nature of this danger and its serious implications, it is necessary to know the function and nature of the ear and how it operates. Only thus can we appreciate the vital importance it has in one's life.

We have an outer acoustic ear which registers sounds and an interior ear which receives images; similarly we have an outer eye which optically senses visible objects and an inner eye which captures images. The outer ear differentiates in order to know, gathers and processes data, measures, analyzes, and recognizes. Its task is conceptual and quantitative. It concerns itself with the contingent. The interior ear, on the contrary, totalizes in order to understand. It receives sound images whose meaning is total and inexhaustible. Its function is perceptual and qualitative; it is concerned with the transcendental.

The transcendental, inaudible and ineffable content of a rhythmic flow of sound images at high frequency can only be captured and understood by the inner ear by coming into resonance with them. Not much is known of the nature of the phenomenon of resonance; it does not belong to the three dimensions of space and time.

Things and beings enter into mutual resonance because they are in a certain harmonic relationship, not because they are simultaneous or contiguous. For Schopenhauer, the universe is "the incarnation of music." Ancient myths bear poetic testimony to the materialization of a sound energy, creator and destroyer of form, which in obedience to musical principles emerges from primordial Silence to create the universe.

The function of the inner ear is to enter into resonance with the Supreme Spirit, with the ineffable, inaudible Word, experience which demands an attitude of interior silence, attention, obedience and prayer.

The manifestations of the Spirit assume an inexhaustible variety of original forms, all having the same meaning and purpose: reorient us towards the fount of life and eternal youth, re-establish our connection with the Holy Grail, with the center, "the still point of the turning world," by projecting on the homogeneous domesticity of our daily lives something completely different, something of a different quality, the Presence of the Sacred. Without this point of reference, no existential orientation is possible.

On this theme of the respective hierarchy of ear and eye, Plato in *Phaedrus,* in his Dialogues, offers us something of great significance:

"*Socrates:* At the Egyptian city of Naucratis, there was a famous old god, whose name was Theuth; the bird which is called the Ibis is sacred to him, and he was the inventor of many arts, such as arithmetic calculation and geometry, and astronomy and draughts and dice, but his greatest discovery was the use of letters. Now in those days the god Thamus was the king of the whole country of Egypt; and he dwelt in that great city of Upper Egypt which the Hellenes call Egyptian Thebes, and the god himself is called by them Ammon. To him came Theuth and shewed his inventions, desiring that the other Egyptians might be allowed to have the benefit of them; he enumerated them, and Thamus enquired about their several uses, and praised some of them and censured others, as he approved or disapproved of them. It would take a long time to repeat all that Thamus said to Theuth in praise or blame of the various arts. But when they came to letters, 'This,' said Theuth, 'will make the Egyptians wiser and give them better memories; it is a specific both for the memory and for the wit.' Thamus replied: "O most ingenious Theuth, the parent or inventor of an art is not always the best judge of the utility or inutility of his own inventions to the users of them. And in this instance, you who are the father of letters, from a paternal love of your own children have been led to attribute to them a quality which they cannot have; for this discovery of yours will create forgetfulness in the learners' souls, because they will not use their memories; they will trust to the external written character and not remember of themselves. The specific thing which you have discovered is an aid not to memory, but to reminiscence, and you give your disciples not truth, but only the semblance of truth; they will be hearers of many things and will have learned nothing; they will be tiresome company, having the show of wisdom without the reality.'

Phaedrus: Yes, Socrates, you can easily invent tales of Egypt or of any other country.

Socrates: There was a tradition in the temple of Dodona that oaks first gave prophetic utterances. Men of old, unlike in their simplicity to you young philosophers, deemed that if they heard the truth even from 'oak or rock,' it was enough for them; whereas you seem to consider not whether a thing is or is not true, but who the speaker is and from what country the tale comes.

Phaedrus: I acknowledge the justice of your rebuke; and I think that the Theban is right in his views about letters.

Socrates: He would be a very simple person, and quite a stranger to the oracles of Thamus or Ammon, who should leave in writing or receive in writing any art under the idea that the written word would be intelligible or certain."

The falling into disuse of the inner ear and the priority of the eye over the ear has had very serious consequences for humanity.

a) Oral tradition has been replaced by the written and printed word.

b) Word and action have ceased to be synonymous. We are no longer true to our words.

c) People have lost the Pentecostal language of their first world (the given Word), indispensable for real communication.

d) There exists an increasing incapacity for the instant perception of totality as manifested by myth, symbol and image, and also for the perception of gesture motivating action.

e) Loss of contact with the exemplary gestures of the gods and with the paradigmatic models for action; consequently people invent aberrant actions, arising from their own initiative.

f) Increasing intolerance of silence and of being alone with oneself.

g) The literal use and interpretation of words has replaced poetic musical perception and expression. Words used literally can transmit information but are not transcendental. At present, the Word as it appears in the New Testament is read by many Christian priests to their parishioners as if they were reading the newspaper . . . as information. Their inner ear and their musicality has not been cultivated to be able to read with rhythmic musical fluency capable of channeling and transmitting its transcendent content and sacred quality.

For this state of things, we, the musicians are largely
responsible. What today we call musical education is mostly
concerned with acquiring techniques and information and with
the training of the outer ear and eye. It subjects the student to an
external direction of expression which impedes his free obedience
to the exigencies of the real which can only manifest itself
through an authentic artistic expression of the "given." The
students study the score, repeating it until it fatigues and bores
them in order to note perfect and automate their performance.
Finally they no longer hear the work and the quality of its sounds.
As music lies beyond the score, the student working in this way
never crosses the threshold of it. For music to appear, the work
should never be repeated but reactualized, always played or sung
expressively as if for the first, last and only time. It must not be
practiced or rehearsed, and much less in fragments. What matters is not the perfect repetition of the score but the adequate
attitude of the musician and the uninterrupted flow of sound
images, bearers of meaning . . . not the music, but what the music
transmits through the musician. The only study a student usually
makes of the origins and nature of music is limited to its historical
and anecdotal aspect which contributes nothing to the understanding of musical experience which is not historic, but transcendental and ineffable. Imagination is not taken into account.

With such a preparation, it is not surprising to find that
the majority of professional musicians in general know nothing of
the true nature, function and reason for existing of music and its
mode of operation. By extension, this situation has produced
serious confusion and disorientation in the general public whose
birthright is musical experience—the necessity to make music for
themselves—since this is the most direct natural means of preserving physical and mental health.

By making of music a profession, we have convinced
people that in order to have access to serious musical experience,
one must be specially gifted and submit oneself to a long process
of technical training which necessarily produces a sterilization of
the imagination. To make music by ear is not considered serious.

The ancient Athenians were only too aware of the dangers
implicit in professionalism and specialization. As H. D. F. Kitto
points out in *The Greeks* (Penguin): "As far as possible every

citizen participated in the affairs of the *polis*, turning his hand to any task that fell to him. In this way everyone was familiar with public affairs. For the Athenians this was not so much a question of social obligation but one of educational privilege—for it implied self-discipline and development and vital responsibility. The professional was accounted of lower standing; the expert was generally a public slave."

Naturally such a system of self-government in which everyone participates on an equal standing cannot be maintained except in a limited community, something which became only too self-evident in the experimental school we established in La Plata. Any appreciable increase in numbers forcibly produces a demand for professional experts—and a complete change of attitude. The developing and maturation of the individual through creative participation is no longer the focus of attention. What matters are the public affairs themselves. The individual becomes a mere spectator, governed by others, a cipher in a mass population. Nowadays the amateur, whether in music or in other skills, now occupies the position once held by the professional under the old Athenian regime.

17 *The Nature and Value of Silence*

Sound energy operating sacramentally in a sacred context creates form; this same energy acting profanely in a profane context destroys form. Sound therefore is not innocuous; it cannot be used indiscriminately. Creative sound emerges from a sacred fount of origin submerged in primordial silence and darkness.

It is this silence and darkness (free of all preconceptions) that musicians must reactualize within themselves in order that the first sound may appear. The sounds the musicians produce must have the same transparency, buoyancy and resonance as the primordial sound. Only thus can they produce sound images through which Reality can manifest itself without impediment.

In order to produce this quality of sound, with their voice or on an instrument, musicians must assume the creative gesture of the *homo religiosus*, and attune the inner ear to the birth of each sound at the precise instant in which they break into silence. With this sound and silence he or she must then reactualize the creation of a sonorous, mythical, poetical world by a rhythmic projection of sound images into an ocean of silence. In these images, both sound and silence are present. Silence and sound form a rhythmic continuum through which flows what reality transmits on making itself manifest. The musician must be just as attentive to silence as to sound.

Usually we only think of silence when voices of authority remind us that the lack of silence is the cause of serious illness. We know more about its absence than about its presence. Today, the majority of people, members of a sick community, cannot tolerate silence. However, humanity today has an urgent necessity to reincorporate silence into daily life. Silence is the essential element for communication with others, with oneself and with Being.

117

The twentieth century prides itself, and rightly so, on its conquests in the development of communications, for it has technically united the world. But it ignores the tragic reality of the existence of an essential lack of human communication on a scale never known before. The literalness to which we have reduced verbal expression and reception has recreated the tower of Babel, and true communication amongst people is harder than ever before.

For Plotinus, the need to speak is the sanction of a fall which has deprived us of our original perfection. Such a necessity disappears on a higher level of existence. "As far as language is concerned, one must not suppose that the beings use it whilst belonging to the intelligible world, or whilst their bodies are in heaven. In the intelligible world, there exist none of the necessities or uncertainties which here below compel us to exchange words. The beings who act normally and in accordance with Nature have no order or advice to give; they all know each other by pure intelligence. Even here below, we know men by sight without need of speech. But there on a higher plane, everybody is pure; each one is like an eye, nothing is hidden or simulated." (Enneads LV, 3,18)

We know from experience that these two levels of existence, sacred and profane, are the option that life offers us on this earth. The profane man's reading of the landscape is verbal and literal, whereas that of the *homo religiosus* is silent, operating through the resonance of an image in his inner ear and eye. The image is transparent and reveals everything. The image of an individual is the projection of his gesture. The reading of the landscape by image and gesture reveals and preannounces the intention of all actions.

Referring to this, Gusdorf in *Speaking* says: "I can only manifest the exterior, the surface of my thoughts. Their depth always evades expression, because the depth does not consist of ideas or objects but of the attitude which characterizes the intention of my whole life. This aspect of my being cannot be made explicit, and yet it is in relation to it that the sense of all I can say is established. Therefore I cannot make public the best of me; and to the degree in which no two existences can be totally coincident, I have no sure means of connecting myself with the best of another. So every man remains a secret for everyone else. There can be no direct agreement or complete understanding. The master offers his disciples his teachings, but his expressed, objective doctrine is not the best of his influence. Apart from what is said, and in spite of it, a dialogue establishes itself between master and disciple, a wordless dialogue, a secret dialogue, different each time, and the only decisive one.

"The explicit teaching of the master is much less important than the testimony of his attitude, the charm of a gesture or a smile. The rest is silence, for the ultimate magistral word of a man is not a term. The most authentic communication between human beings is not the spoken word, that is to say it operates in spite of language, fortuitously and often in a sense contrary to that expressed by language. The last refuge within each one of us is a kingdom to which words have no access. Silence is more authentic than words."

Ivan Illich (*Awareness*) in turn observes: "The science of linguistics has opened up new horizons for human communication. An objective study of the modes of transmitting meanings demonstrates that far more is communicated from one man to another by means of silence than by word of mouth. Sentences are composed of words and silences, silences being more significant than words. The gravid pauses between sounds and expressions transform themselves into luminous points in an incredible void: like electrons in the atom, like planets in the solar system. Language is a thread of silence in which the sounds form the knots—like the knots in the Peruvian *quipu*—and where it is the empty spaces that are eloquent. With Confucius we can see language as a wheel. The spokes centralize, but the empty spaces constitute the wheel.

"It is not so much the words of another that we must learn in order to understand him, but rather his silences. It is through the medium of our pauses that we make ourselves understood, rather than our sounds. To learn a language is more a question of learning its silences than its sounds. Only the Christian believes in the Word as coeternal silence. Amongst men living in time, rhythm constitutes a law by which our speech converts itself into a yin-yang of sound and silence.

"Therefore to learn a language in a human mature way is to accept the responsibility for its silences and its sounds. The gift which a people makes us by teaching us its language is more the gift of the rhythm, mode and subtleties of its system of silences."

No doubt St. Bernard would have subscribed to the words of St. John of the Cross: "The Father spoke one Word which was His Son, who spoke always in eternal silence, and in silence must be heard by the soul," since for him, silence, inner and outer, was an indispensable condition to be able to hear and connect with truth. "The temple conceived by St. Bernard was an authentic oratory where man, in silence and penumbra, could synthesize and listen to Heaven, elaborating as food and bread the Word-Seed of the Divine Verb." (Larcher)

From the *Upanishads* comes the same warning as from St. Bernard:

> *There is something which lies beyond the mind and which abides in silence. It is the Supreme Mystery which transcends thought. One must allow the mind and the subtle body to repose in this "something" and on nothing else.*

— Maita Upanishad

> *When the five senses and the mind are at rest and reason itself reposes in silence, it is then the Supreme Road begins.*

— Katha Upanishad

> *When the mind becomes silent, beyond all weakness and distraction, it is then it can enter into a world beyond the mind, in the Supreme End.*

— Maitri Upanishad

18 *Sound, Voice and Song*

Let us now return once again to our previous point of reference, the myths of the Creation, in order to observe how the original creative sound organized itself rhythmically into songs which finally materialized into the created world. We human beings are the materialization of these rhythmic sonorous songs. In the great process of the creation of the universe, sound, rhythm, songs and the voice play the principal roles. The basic experience of the musician then, should be spontaneous song, something which at present is far from being the case. By the experience of his own voice, raised in an attitude or prayer, megalithic man was able to formulate his myths of the Creation.

Marius Schneider tells us that "this sonorous force was considered by the cosmogonies of the superior megalithic cultures (specially through commentaries such as the Upanishads) as the fundamental substance of all the forces of the Universe. It was the oneiric substance (Traumsubstanz) from which the whole world emerged originally.

"Both in traditional and superior cultures we very frequently find the idea that this original music of the Creation reappears at the birth of each individual, sounding slightly different for each creature. But it culminates in the conviction that this dream music, in its occasionally different tonality, not only constitutes the essence of each individual, but connects this essence with the primitive era, with the singing age of dream or oneiric time in which its bearer or interpreter is rooted.

"This high estimation of sound energy is at the same time recognizable in the rites, whose songs constitute the substance of the acts and are the bridges (Grenzsubstanz) to that region of dream in which our ancestors localized the fount of life."

It is most important to stress the extraordinary importance that song has always had within the rites, whether primitive or cultured . . . song, understood as the most direct, spontaneous and efficacious mode of praying, is the axis of the rite.

St. Bernard, in the instruction he gave to his monks, made special reference to the way Gregorian plainchant should be sung in his oratories. In this he reactualizes the ancestral beliefs about ritual song. He reduced and prohibited the excessive prolongation of the melismas, since for him Gregorian chant was above all "a means of transport, a direct road of access to the Creator. Pre-Christian symbolism would have called it a *cart*, or a *ship* or a *river* in which luminous sonorous syllables transport themselves. Feeling is not its body and origin, but only its shadow and sequel."

The myths show us our true relation to sound. Far from being something extraneous to us, to be used indiscriminately for various purposes, it constitutes our very essence, for we are born of sound and are the incarnation of it. They also show us that for this very reason, each individual "sounds" within the universal concert: a fundamental sound with all its harmonics sustaining an individual melody or song.

Schneider says that "the fundamental sound is the protoplasm of the vital energy of a man. It constitutes the ultimate metaphysical and individual reality of its bearer. The individual song is one that expresses each one's individual rhythm and is inimitable.

"The Biblical phase 'In the beginning was the Word' would seem to belong to the most ancient ideological treasure of humanity. Even the Uitotes, totemic tribes of the American forest, say: 'In the beginning the Verb gave birth to the Father'; by Father they mean the Supreme God. Now the term Verb or Word is nothing more than a more or less adequate linguistic expedient for formulating an idea almost inaccessible to verbal intelligence and human language, since the term is used to indicate something supralogical which is anterior and superior to any defined notion, clearly limited. According to Egyptian mythology, the world is born of the creative cry of the god Thot. The Vedic tradition tells us of a sound (a more general and less limited phenomenon than any particular sound) from the immateriality of which emerged the world, born of nothing, through the progressive materialization of the initial sonorous rhythm. This rhythm subsists today in the mystic syllable *Om*, sonorous symbol of the Creation and synonymous with *arrow*.

"The voice is man." The voice is revealing and impossible to dissemble. For those who can hear with their inner ear, the voice is the faithful reflection of its bearer. "Song is the soul and is its vehicle. There exists a sonorous thread (one of whose extremities is constituted by the earth) that establishes a bridge between the creator and human beings, between metaphysical and physical reality, situated between the world of eternity and our world of appearances, and in the form of a spiral it traverses all the region of dreams woven by the material world of our illusions.

"This sonorous route has remained untouched by the partial materialization of the acoustic world. It has persisted till the present day, just as it emerged from the primordial abysm, that is to say as a singing tree.

"Access to it, which was easy during the first era of the Creation, has now become more difficult because it is invisible from the material world. Furthermore, this bridge between heaven and earth is not transitable except with an extraordinary degree of confidence."

Schneider then tells us how human beings gradually set a distance between themselves and the gods (a process to which Eliade also refers). They ceased to value and utilize this bridge of sound "and even felled the singing tree within them, the umbilical cord which united them to Heaven. So fatal was the result of this loss of a direct connection with the gods, that a civilizing hero and redeemer had to descend from Heaven to teach people the precise songs and rites for recuperating their immortality. This venerated benefactor, often a mythical ancestor, made men understand that in this materialized world the offering of his vital breath by singing was the most direct, certain and efficacious way of returning to the bridge, the thread and the ladder which unites Heaven and earth.

"The gods are not indifferent to the sonorous sacrifices which people offer them, because these rites affect the very substance of the immortals. They are compelled to participate. Human beings cannot elude the sacrifice that the gods demand, but they are free to accept it by singing or turn a deaf ear and remain mute and passive. The sacrifice is mutual. It is the law of the world. But when it is sonorous, the gods materialize and men spiritualize on this road, and thus is accomplished the interpenetration of Heaven and earth."

In another paragraph, Schneider reactualizes the thesis of St. Bernard: "In the measure that man is willing to transform himself into a resonator, into a 'fine ear,' he is recompensed by the power to withdraw the veil of illusion and approach the acoustic world of the dead. The sonorous sacrifice is superior to all other forms of sacrifice. It is the substance of ritual song and resounds in the vibrant string (thread or bridge), in the flute (the bamboo footbridge), or in the drum (the singing tree)."

19 *Expression*

Expression is a common word in a musician's vocabulary, but in a music student's preparation no serious attempt is usually made to discover its meaning and implications. The students, left to their own devices, either ignore the question or make the wildest guesses and assumptions. How often have I heard an inquisitive student being told: "Don't worry about that; you are here to learn the techniques of your profession. After that, if you have anything to say you will express yourself." And that would be the final word on the subject. I, as a professional, was as ignorant as my students. It was only after long years of musical exploration and the aid of studies in other disciplines such as those cited in this book, that my students and I began to realize what expression implied. Musicians have nothing to say, only something to transmit. They must make of themselves a well-tuned instrument on which Reality can play. They must turn their attention inwards and come into ontological resonance with the mythic poetical content of the music employing their inner ear.

In the work done in the musical workshop, one of the basic things we had discovered was the necessity for potentializing one's personality in order to actualize individuality. We live in a society which lays special emphasis on the development of personality. But music is concerned with being, not with personality, and the musician must lay aside everything personal in order to *be* the music and allow a rhythmic flow of sound images to emerge from its mythic content.

Faithful image of the man who transforms himself into a resonator and "fine ear" to become a true musician is this legend taken from Okakura KaKuzo's *Book of Tea*. Peiwoh lays aside everything pertaining to his personality in order to disappear into

125

the mythical landscape of the music. But in spite of and because of this anonymity, Peiwoh becomes individualized as a unique and exceptional musician.

"Once upon a time, in the hoary ages, in the ravine of Lungmen stood a Kiri tree, a veritable king of the forest. It raised its head to converse with the stars; its roots penetrated deep into the earth, mingling their bronzed coils with those of the silver dragon that slept beneath. And it came to pass that a mighty wizard made of this tree a wondrous harp, whose stubborn spirit could only be tamed by the greatest of musicians.

"For a long time the instrument was treasured by the Emperor of China, but all in vain were the efforts of those who in turn tried to draw melody from its strings. In response to their greatest efforts there came from the harp but harsh notes of disdain, ill-according with the songs they wished to sing. The harp refused to recognize a master.

"Finally came Peiwoh, the prince of harpists. With tender hand he caressed the harp, as one might seek to soothe an unruly horse, and softly touched the chords. He sang of nature and the seasons, of high mountains and flowing waters, and all the memories of the tree awoke! Once more the sweet breath of spring played amidst its branches. The cataracts, as they danced down the ravine, laughed to the budding flowers. Anon were heard the dreamy voices of summer with its myriad insects, the gentle pattering of rain, the wail of the cuckoo. Hark! a tiger roars—the valley answers again. It is autumn; in the desert night, sharp as a sword, gleams the moon upon the frosted grass. Now winter reigns, and through the snow-filled air swirl flocks of swans, and rattling hailstones beat upon the boughs with fierce delight.

"Then Peiwoh changed the key and sang of love. The forest swayed like an ardent swain deep lost in thought. On high, like a haughty maiden, swept a cloud bright and fair; but passing, trailed long shadows on the ground, black like despair. Again the mood was changed; Peiwoh sang of war, of clashing steel and trampling steeds. And in the harp arose the tempest of Lungmen, the dragon rode the lightning, the thundering avalanche crashed through the hills. In ecstasy the Celestial monarch asked Peiwoh wherein lay the secret of his victory. 'Sire,' he replied, 'others have failed because they sang but of themselves. I left the harp to choose its theme, and knew not truly whether the harp had been Peiwoh or Peiwoh were the Harp.'"

At the present time, how many apparent musicians of great renown fail for the same reason; they are only concerned with and sing of themselves, instead of making of themselves a resonator and a "fine ear." With great virtuosity they emit opaque aggressive sounds, totally lacking in resonance and affectivity and therefore inadequate for musical purposes, for they can transmit nothing. No Reality can manifest itself through sounds of this profane quality. So deep is the sleep into which modern society has fallen, and the amnesia from which it suffers, that this question is totally ignored in the formation of a musician.

Those who, pretending to be musicians, are opaque and incapable of resounding in reality, reduce their audiences to mere spectators present at a concert in which they have no means of participating. All they can do is concentrate their attention on the score, the technique and the executant.

When the true musician, the authentic resonator appears, everything changes immediately. Everyone begins to participate and nourish himself physically and spiritually with the affective "manna" of reality which the musician channels. The musicians and their hearers experience a plentitude of being, a joy of living, that revives in them the nostalgia for Paradise lost and provides them with the experience of being reborn and arising from their own ashes.

Then, and only then, do music and the musician accomplish their true function. What matters is not the correctness of notes and techniques but to establish and maintain an uninterrupted flow of significant sound images through the singing string or bridge, bearer of meaning and affectivity. In such a situation, applause is absurd and desacralizing, as it would be if we went to Mass and applauded the officiating priests. As Mircea Eliade observes, "by experiencing the sacred, the human mind comes to understand the difference between what reveals itself as real, powerful, rich and significant, and that which is not—for instance, the chaotic dangerous flow of things, their appearances and disappearances and their senselessness. The experience of the sacred reveals existence, meaning and truth."

In order to establish a sacred nexus with audiences, musicians must allow the music to play them and not the reverse. They must set aside that single technique applicable to all situations. Each occasion requires a different technique (techne for the Greeks) adequate only for that particular moment, and in which is implicit the gesture of inner obedience of the musician to the expressive exigencies of the music.

Music can only appear in the eternal present, for it is a sacred manifestation. We live in a profane society governed by profane chronological time which passes fragmented into past and future. We feed on memories and illusory projects. For us the apparition of the present is the irruption of the sacred into the fearful instant that passes never to return, but is nevertheless eternally recoverable by reactualizing it through rites. It is the instant in which a unified space-time appears with the quality of eternal present. In this space-time, as T.S. Eliot says, music does not pass away:

> Words move, music moves
> Only in time; but that which is only living
> Can only die. Words, after speech, reach
> Into the silence. Only by the form, the pattern,
> Can words or music reach
> The stillness, as a Chinese jar still
> Moves perpetually in its stillness.
> Not the stillness of the violin, while the note lasts,
> Not that only, but the co-existence,
> Or say that the end precedes the beginning,
> And the end and the beginning were always there,
> Before the beginning and after the end.
> And all is always now.

— T.S. Eliot *The Four Quartets*

When the poet speaks of the form of music he is not referring to the structure of the score but to the symbolic form of its unwritten inexhaustible content. Albert Gleizes, in his *La forme et l'histoire*, refers to this matter, showing us how aboriginal people employ tattooing to disintegrate their figures in order to enter into significant form. He also draws our attention to the two opposite attitudes adopted by human beings across the centuries, as shown by his artistic creations:

a) They make of themselves prominent figures, outstanding against a contrasting background.

b) They disappear into the landscape to become an integral part of it.

When musicians obey themselves by coming into resonance with reality, this intimate symbolic musical form is always new. Drawing in the way described on page 15, I have worked many, many times with the same theme and obtained as many different forms, all transmitting the same meaning. Naturally when playing or singing in identical conditions, the same thing occurs.

It is therefore absurd to impose on music a preconceived, temporal and external form by rigorous rehearsals. Each time we play or sing a work, it must assume, for once only, a new and unforeseeable form, that which emerges from the strict inner expressive obedience, from the sonorous sacrifice of each individual. It is equally obvious that musical expression cannot be directed.

The context of the flow of sonorous images which music offers us is symbolic and mythical. The meanings transmitted by myth, symbol and image are infinite and inexhaustible; the mythical hero has a thousand faces but always serves the same purpose: redirect and connect to the Center through intimate resonance with the intersection of time and eternity. The symbolic forms of music appear in my drawings as expressive energy forms which resound in me when my inner obedience is at the necessary level.

The temporal form or structure of music is the container or scaffolding of its essential significant form. This interior form cannot be seen or heard except by coming into resonance with the rhythmic flow of myth symbol and image. This rhythmic flow cannot constitute itself in profane chronological time where opaque, differentiated sounds can only accumulate, add up, not fuse: A + B + C. In sacred space-time, on the contrary, sounds fuse in a process of genesis, in which A gives birth to B and AB to C . . . etc. In the first case, however brilliant the execution, the work transmits nothing.

In musical spheres we make free use of the word interpretation which is totally disorienting, for in music there is nothing to be interpreted. Musicians must let the flow of sound images project themselves through them without any interference on their part. Their origin is mythical and not of personal invention. They come as a gift to them and the music emerges fresh and original from the source of Being.

The same work "interpreted" or "transmitted" produces two irreconcilable versions, unmusical or musical. But musical deafness has now become so generalized that we are losing our capacity to discriminate between them.

20 *The Nature and Experience of Image*

Both the creation and reception of sound images depend on a direct connection with the center. Gaston Bachelard (*The Poetics of Space*) tells us that in order to gain access to the image, we, who have been brought up in a society dominated by an active and ever-increasing rationalism, must set aside all our information and prejudices and break with all our habits. "Here the cultural past is of no account; the long effort to connect and give structure to thought is inefficacious. One has to be present, present in the image, in the instant of the image." Here we must bear in mind that all true artistic images channel and project a poetic-mythic content; that what is true of the images to be found in poetry is equally valid for all artistic images including, naturally, music. The testimony of Bachelard makes an invaluable contribution to the comprehension of the nature of a rhythmic flow of meaningful sound images and how they operate to bring us into resonance with them.

The new poetic image resounds in an archtype, in an innate primordial wisdom sleeping in the depths of the unconscious. But the relation between them, says Bachelard "is not *causal*. Nevertheless, the image is not an echo of the past; it is rather the contrary. The impact of an image causes a far distant past to resound, full of echoes, and it is extremely difficult for one to foresee at what depth such echoes are going to reverberate and extinguish themselves.

"In its novelty, in its activity, the poetic image has a life and dynamism of its own. It emerges directly from an ontology." The image in whatever artistic field it appears, is unique and has a polyvalency. What is true of the poetic image is equally valid for the sonorous image of music, since both emerge from the same original mythical source and operate in the same way.

At the present time, there exists a very generalized belief that in the field of music and in the visual arts, a prolix technical historical knowledge is necessary in order to have access to the works. Nothing could be further removed from reality. Bachelard remarks: "The poet does not confide to me the past of his image and yet his image takes root instantaneously in me." The contact is direct, without the intervention of any explanation. In any case, the image is not explicable.

"*The communicability of a unique image is of great ontological significance.* We renew our contact with it in brief, active and isolated moments. Images—after their first impact—train us; but they are not the product of training. *The image in its simplicity requires no knowledge.* It is not even objectified in the written sounds and words." The literal reading of poetry or of a musical score makes the appearance of an image impossible.

"The image is the gift of an ingenuous consciousness. In its expression it is the birth of language.The poet in the originality of his images is always the origin of language. The image is always previous to thought."

Herbert Read (*Image and Idea*) makes an important observation with reference to this:

"If the image always precedes the idea in the development of human consciousness, as I maintain it does, not only must we rewrite the history of culture, but also revise all the postulates of our philosophies. And above all, we must ask ourselves once again, what are the correct principles of education?"

Returning now to the testimony of Bachelard, he says that "For a simple poetic image there exists no project. All that is necessary is a movement of the soul. In a poetic image the soul announces its presence." For his part Mircea Eliade points out "that today we understand something of which in the nineteenth century there existed not the slightest presentiment: that myth, symbol and image belong to the substance of spiritual life; that they can be camouflaged, mutilated and degraded but never extirpated. Symbolic thought is not something exclusive to children, poets and the unbalanced-minded. It is consubstantial with the human being; it precedes language and discursive reason. Symbols reveal certain aspects of reality—the most profound—not accessible to any other means of knowledge.

"Images, by their very structure, possess multivalency. If the spirit employs them in order to apprehend the ultimate reality of things, it is precisely because this reality manifests itself in such a contradictory way that it cannot be expressed in concepts. An image, as such, as an inexhaustible nucleus of meanings, is what is true, and not any single one of its meanings or planes of reference. To translate an image into a concrete terminology, reducing it to a single plane of reference, is worse than mutilating it; it destroys and annuls it as an instrument of knowledge."

A valuable image for us are the Eskimo. Edmund Carpenter makes a study of them in *Eskimo* and in *Eskimo Realities*. I feel that his most valuable contribution to the understanding of these peoples has been his insight, his capacity to penetrate beyond facts and actions to the quality of the gestures and life attitudes inspiring them. He was thus able to perceive what for many well-intentioned invaders passed unnoticed, namely the uprooting of the Eskimos from their original mythical world and the existential havoc wrought by the imposition of a contemporary desacralized mode of existence. "Amongst the Aivelik Eskimo, the binding force of oral tradition is so strong that the eye is dominated by the ear. In the beginning there was the Word, not the visual word of the educated man, but the word which when pronounced imposes form. The word is also operative for the Eskimo, but with a significant difference: the Eskimo poet does not impose form, he reveals it. He transfigures and clarifies and thus sanctifies. When he speaks, the form emerges fugacious, but clearly, 'on the threshold of his tongue.'"

My drawings, some of which appear in Chapter 4, are an attempt to make visible the expressive forms music and poetry generate in me. It is through the medium of these forms that I become the musical or poetical image.

"The land on which the Eskimo live is snowbound for the greater part of the year. It never unfreezes. Life is thus reduced to the minimum necessities; art and poetry are two of them. In Eskimo the word for 'making poetry' is the term 'to breathe'—both derive from anerca, the soul, that which is eternal. A poem is a group of words infused with breath and spirit. 'Let me breathe it,' says the poet, and then adds, 'I have put my poem on the threshold of my tongue.'

"I call this song 'My breath,' said Orpingalik, 'because it is just as necessary for me to sing it as to breathe. We are afraid to use words; but it happens that the words we need emerge spontaneously.When the words appear spontaneously, we have a new song.' When Orpingalik says he is afraid to use words he does not mean he is afraid of words, but that he goes in holy terror of their power to bring the universe into existence. The words must appear of their own accord, arise spontaneously from experience. To impose one's own words would be sacrilege. 'Many are the words that pass swiftly over me, like the wings of birds coming out of the darkness. How many songs I have I cannot say,' said Orpingalik. 'I don't keep count of such things. There are so many occasions in one's life when joy or grief is felt so intensely that there surges up a desire to sing; so all I know is that I have many songs. All my being is a song and I sing as I breathe.'"

Bachelard speaks of resonances and reverberations. "The resonances of an image disperse themselves amongst the different planes of our life in the world; the reverberations convoke us to a more profound existence. In the resonances we understand the poem, in the reverberations we speak to it, it is ours. The reverberations produce a change of direction of our being. The poem takes total possession of us. The reverberation of a single poetic image can produce a real awakening of poetic creation in us, by mobilizing all our linguistic activity and situating us in the origins of the speaking individual.

"We feel a poetical capacity arise ingenuously within us . . . the image has stirred the depths without perturbing the surface. This image that the reading of a poem offers us suddenly becomes ours. It takes root in us. We have received it, but we feel we could and should have created it. It becomes a new element of our language; it expresses us by making us be what it expresses. In other words it is simultaneously the activity of expression and that of our being. Here expression creates being.

"The image concentrates being within the limits which protect it. It sets us at the limit where the function of the Real is precisely to seduce or disquiet—but always to awaken—the human being asleep in his automatisms.

"The speaking subject must be totally present within the poetical image, for unless he surrenders himself to it completely, he will be unable to enter into the poetic space of the image"; or, as René Huyh says: "One must cast oneself into the Center, into the heart, into the round point where everything originates and has its meaning."

And C. G. Jung in *The Secret of the Golden Flower* tells us that "the image facilitates and maintains the direction of the attention, or rather the participation, inwards towards the interior precinct, original objective of the soul, which contains that unity of life and consciousness which man once possessed, then lost, and now must find again."

Two poets testify to this experience of being in the Center of the image, St. John of the Cross and T.S. Eliot.

> *I knew not where I entered*
> *but finding myself there*
> *not knowing where I was*
> *great things I understood.*
> *I cannot say what I felt*
> *for I remained unknowing*
> *all science transcending.*
>
> *This knowing without knowledge*
> *is of so great a power*
> *that the learned, arguing,*
> *can never surpass it;*
> *for all their knowledge cannot attain*
> *to this knowing without knowing*
> *all science transcending.*
>
> *Of such great excellence*
> *is this supreme knowledge,*
> *that there is no faculty or science*
> *that with it can compare;*
> *he who can conquer himself*
> *with this unknowing knowledge,*
> *will forever transcend.*

And if you would know,
this supreme science
consists of a certain
feeling for the Divine Essence.
It is the work of his clemency
to make us remain unknowing
all science transcending.

— St. John of the Cross

How well I know the fount
that springs and flows
        although it is night.

That eternal fount is hidden,
well I know from where it springs
        although it is night.

Its origin I know not, for it has none,
but I know that all origin from it comes
        although it is night.

I know that its waters are so abundant
that they water hell, heaven, and the people,
        although it is night.

This eternal fount is hidden
in this live bread to give us life
        although it is night.

Here all creatures are being called upon
To satiate themselves with this water,
        although in darkness
        although it is night.

— St. John of the Cross

At the still point of the turning world. Neither flesh nor fleshless;
Neither from nor towards; the still point, there the dance is,
But neither arrest nor movement. And do not call it fixity,
Where past and future are gathered. Neither movement from nor
> *towards,*
Neither ascent nor decline. Except for the point, the still point,
There would be no dance, and there is only the dance.
I can only say, there *we have been: but I cannot say where.*
And I cannot say, how long, for that is to place it in time.
> *The inner freedom from the practical desire,*
The release from action and suffering, release from the inner
And the outer compulsion, yet surrounded
By a grace of sense, a white light still and moving,
Erhebung *without motion, concentration*
Without elimination, both a new world
And the old made explicit, understood
In the completion of its partial ecstasy,
The resolution of its partial horror.

— T.S. Eliot *The Four Quartets*

21 *Fundamental Energy and Matter*

If music is created and comes to us through a rhythmic flow of sound images with which we come into resonance by vibrating in unison with it, it is all-important for us to know something more of ourselves as entities of sound energy in a sonorous universe, to recapture our cosmic dimension, for in the last instance this is what makes music possible and efficacious. For this reason my students and I worked through the two following studies of George de la Warr and Stéphane Lupasco. We were not looking for scientific information but rather sought to get a feeling for basic principles ordering and maintaining our identity as unique entities of energy-matter. They represent two different approaches to the same question, and for us contributed to a fuller comprehension of ourselves as sonorous energy patterns in a state of precarious equilibrium, while helping to restore to music its cosmic dimension and efficacy.

De la Warr says, in what may seem to us unfamiliar terms, what the old myths have already told us. But we are so accustomed to thinking of ourselves exclusively as solid opaque matter, as finite mortals of flesh and bone, that we find it extremely difficult to imagine ourselves in terms of cosmic energy, which is operating in and around everything created.

In 1956, a new and strange study appeared in the form of a book entitled *New Worlds Beyond the Atom*, written by Langston Day in collaboration with George de la Warr, and published in New York by Devin Adair. In this book, Langston Day relates, in synthesis, the investigations of George de la Warr, an English engineer, and his fruitless efforts to interest orthodox medical authorities in them. De la Warr, working in Oxford with his group of collaborators, dedicated long years of investigation to the phenomenon of the subtle radiations emitted by matter at all levels, including the human. He attempted to bring into the field of scientific investigation many phenomena of energy known and used for thousands of years by traditional rural communities. Goethe was one of the first to reactualize this knowledge. Amongst de la Warr's predecessors we find Baron von Reichenbach, of whose works Von Humboldt had said: "The facts are undeniable; it is now the task of science to explain them." There was also a North American doctor, Abrams, who maintained that all matter emits radiations and that the human body can be used as a receiver for them. He discovered that each one of its organs acts individually as a station for radio transmission, emitting waves of a precise frequency when not weak or in ill-health. He claimed that illness was the alteration of this frequency. He further claimed that he could rectify this alteration with an apparatus of his own invention, and also make a diagnosis of the health of a patient by studying the frequencies emitted by his blood specimen.

All these studies seem to have had a profound influence on de la Warr since he, going his own way, continued them. In order to do so, he invented and constructed, as necessity demanded, a series of apparatus to register and reproduce what he calls the subtle radiations emanating from matter and also to make visible the forms inherent in these frequencies.

De la Warr found that the cells of plants emitted some form of radiation when stimulated by sound, and that this radiation was related to the static electricity generated in these cells. He imagined if the plants were treated with sound waves of the same frequency as the modulation of the radiations they emitted, then the plants should resonate and grow faster. Experimentation showed his surmise to be correct. The phenomenon of resonance was a prime factor in all of de la Warr's work.

In May 1950, a scientific and technical congress for Radionics and Radioesthesia was held in London. De la Warr and his collaborators gave lectures on their work and formulated, for the first time, four new laws of physics:

1. The fundamental energy of the universe, in the form of charged particles, manifests through any energy

pattern which modulates it in accordance with the
Law of Harmonic Relation.

2. All forms of matter irradiate a form of combined wave
   of energy which creates a Force Field Body due to the
   interaction of inherent radiations.

3. This Force Field Body is related to atomic structure,
   and acts as a structured complex aerial through which
   Fundamental energy manifests opportunely as matter.

4. The wave form of the modulation which depends on
   factors of time-space can have wave characteristics.

The laws refer to Fundamental Energy or Universal Mind
which, being beyond space and time, is "everywhere" and "always." It is a boundless ocean of potential energy imperceptible
to us, unless we evoke it, within our world of sensory perception;
it then appears to us as some perceptible form of energy or as
matter. This coincides with Einstein's General Theory of Relativity which says that matter and energy are different aspects of
something which is at the same time the origin of both; he also says
that energy is convertible into matter and vice versa.

Form and pattern are the channel through which the
Fundamental Energy manifests itself. Without this "something"
that sustains and vitalizes all forms of matter, both animated and
inanimate, as the ocean sustains marine life, the universe would
be dead and non-existent. But owing to its presence, everything is
alive and emits radiations.

Amongst other things, de la Warr's experiments had
indicated that the elements emit Fundamental Rays oriented to
different points of the compass like the beams of light in a light-
house, or the spokes of a wheel. The Fundamental Rays of atoms,
molecules, cells, etc. combine to constitute the Fundamental Ray
of a larger and more complex organism. This Fundamental Ray is
the final result of one's experience up to the present. To acquire
experience, one must pass through significant happenings. Experience modifies the intrinsic constitution of the entity and also the
radiation it emits, i.e. its Fundamental Ray. De la Warr says:

> *As nothing in the universe goes through exactly the same*
> *experience, both its intrinsic constitution and its Fundamental*

Ray are unique—although at an atomic level, the differences can be so negligible as to be inconceivable. The Primordial Fount of Energy, in order to be free of all limitation, must create a universe than can actualize all possibilities of existence. The Fundamental Ray of each entity is united to others by resonance, and the slightest modification of this Ray makes an immediate impact on the exterior world. It therefore follows that what matters is what one is.

It is strange to find that de la Warr, investigating scientifically in a twentieth century laboratory, confirms what the old traditional myths told us poetically:

    A. That sound is primordial energy capable of creating and destroying form.

    B. That sound operates permanently in the constitution and maintenance of the existence of everything created.

    C. That we ourselves are not only matter, but also sound entities, each contributing a unique sound to the functional universal concert.

    D. That we form an intrinsic part of this creative energy.

    E. That the mode of operation of sound is through resonances; therefore any sound affects us.

    F. That sound is not innocuous, but powerfully operative.

    G. That sound is not something extraneous, but inherent. It should not be used indiscriminately.

22 *The Organization of Energy-matter*

If we are entities of energy inherent in the immense cosmic activity of primordial energy, it is of great importance to us to know how this energy operates and organizes itself and exactly how it affects us.

For this we shall consult Stéphane Lupasco's *The Three Substances*.

"All knowable objects present themselves to us as a more or less stable association of elements, i.e., atomic systems whose mass, negligible in the peripheral electron, nonexistent in the photon or grain of light, but important in the nucleus (proton, meson, neutron) would continue to be the expression of an old notion of matter, if the relativity of Einstein had not reduced it to the concept of energy.

"Every energy system is the function of antagonistic forces (contradictory, not contrary, for they are inherent in the same antagonism) and the mechanism of the events by which it is constituted. We cannot find a single astrophysical system without forces of attraction and repulsion (even in the relativist synthesis of Einstein), forces which issue from the physical properties themselves of the astronomic objects. Nor do we find any molecular, atomic or nuclear system without forces (of complex modality, no doubt) that unite events, and forces which disperse them. There is no sector of experience or experimentation, macro- or microphysical, that does not show clear evidence of this antagonism, indispensable for the formation of a system.

"All energy not only possesses antagonistic dynamisms, but these dynamisms are, and must be, such that the actualization of one implies the potentialization of the other, or that both meet on the two trajectories of the passage from a potential to an actual

143

state, and from actual to potential towards, or in, a state of equal potentialization and equal actualization.

"It must be pointed out that there exists no experimental system which we can consider simple, primary or elemental, that is to say, composed of a single and final pair of antagonistic dynamisms. Such a system can only exist to meet the necessities of developing a theory or for experimental investigation, which in any case does not allow even a glimpse of any definite limit. Every system reveals itself as a system of systems which comprehends all levels towards the macro- and micro-physical, with no ultimate limits.

"The antagonistic forces that organize these systems are homogenization and heterogenization." Lupasco, studying these ample and complex systems of systems, discerns three different organizations of matter, imposed by the activity of the two antagonistic forces, at different levels. "What is meant by matter is always a systematization of energy, endowed with a certain resistance.

A. *Quantal, microphysical, psychic matter* in which the two antagonistic forces are semi-actualized. This matter, whose strange manifestations are the object of study of Quantum Physics, could not be classified either as animate or inanimate matter, although in many aspects it resembles both.

B. *Live, biological matter* in which the heterogenizing force actualizes itself and the homogenizing force is potentialized. It is macroscopic and consists of living organisms. The science of this matter is still in an empirical state.

C. *Macroscopic inanimate matter* in which the homogenizing force actualizes itself and the heterogenizing force is potentialized.

"That is to say that in A the two antagonistic forces are in a state of precarious equilibrium and we have microphysical psychic matter. In B, where the heterogenizing force is predominant we have live matter. In C, the homogenizing force prevails, and we have macroscopic inanimate matter.

"Everything in this matter of triple aspect reduces itself to energy. The three matters are constituted by the same energetic elements or events or energy systems.

"The psychic system controls the other two energy systems. It is composed of the semi-actualization and the semi-potentialization of both. The soul penetrates with the same force and depth in the two kingdoms of matter (i.e., of energy), although it repels them and separates itself from them. It is necessary to await their coming in order that there shall emerge from energy the permanent and antinomic consciousness of life and death. The soul carries within it these fantastic events that constitute its matter. Everything in the soul can be referred to phenomena of life and phenomena of death and yet it is neither life nor death.

"It is this conflict between the homogenizing and heterogenizing forces which causes the soul to create the antinomic world of myth, for the soul is a crossroads with innumerable opposite directions. Submerged in uniformity, fixity and repetition, the soul tires, becomes bored and dies."

This is the secret of the failure of most of our present systems of education, both general and artistic. Students and teachers are annihilated by the lethal effects of stereotyped uniformity, fixity and repetition.

Lupasco says that "a despotic rationality, a devastating homogenization makes the soul ill and can even destroy it, as certain types of psychosis show. If, on the contrary, the soul cedes to change, to diversity, to the dynamisms of heterogenization, it becomes dislocated and dispersed; it loses itself. In the first case, it is the physical system obeying the laws of inanimate matter, with its own logic (our classical logic) that captures the psychic system and substitutes it. In the second, it is the biological system that seizes upon it and dilates it excessively, and then other psychoses, the opposite of the preceding, appear. The morbid manifestations registered rightly or wrongly in the notions of schizophrenia, cyclothymia, paranoia, catatonia, etc., belong to these two antagonistic classes of psychic disturbance.

"The 'body' itself contains nothing of that which has always been accorded to the notion. The constituent atoms of a live body . . . only remain in the body for a certain time and they all renovate themselves incessantly. This includes the proteins, those substances that were always considered the foundation stones of the edifice, the plastic elements *par excellence*. At the end of a year, the atoms of a human being have been totally renovated, even those which constitute the micro-crystalline substance of the bones.

"What remains is the form, the primary structure, the systematization, in spite of the energetic events which happen and which submit to the laws and directions of the systematization. But this form is broken up continually; it destroys and reconstructs itself incessantly, in its smallest details, in all its chemical reactions. . . .

"We are never masters of our own soul, at any time or place. The soul elaborates and disintegrates itself (under cover of our appearance and our words) to be reborn incessantly, in the same way as our physical and biological systems, in which we die and are reborn continually. Undoubtedly this is the origin of the universal myth of the resurrection."

As an inevitable participant in this eternal process of cosmic death and resurrection, one can discover the profound content of this prayer for initiatory death and rebirth from ancient Egypt:

> Death is in my eyes today,
> like a sick man
> who recovers his health and integrity,
> like walking abroad after illness.
>
> Death is in my eyes today,
> like the fragrance of myrrh,
> like sitting beneath the boat's sail
> on a day of strong breezes
>
> Death is in my eyes today,
> like the smell of water lilies,
> like sitting on the edge of inebriety.
>
> Death is in my eyes today,
> like a well trodden road,
> like a man who returns from campaigning
> in a foreign country.
>
> Death is in my eyes today,
> like the heavens which unveil themselves,

like a man who there accedes
to what he ignored.

Death is in my eyes today,
like the desire of a man to see his home
after long years of captivity.

We, then, are part of this incessant energetic activity of the cosmos, and it affects us at three levels: psychic, biological and physical. Amongst the impetuous impact of this great dance, the function of the psyche is to maintain in us a precarious equilibrium between life and death, between heterogeneity and homogeneity. Our cohesion as a form of life and our individual identities are maintained, furthermore, by a cosmic resonance which operates, like music, within a law of Harmonics. In this way music is intrinsic to our existence.

But far and beyond this permanent state of contingency, there exists in us another level of existence which is immutable: the level of being which participates in the immutability of Being. The psyche, in search of an anchorage for the soul, creates the mouth as a transcendental bridge to connect us with universal and intemporal Reality.

Lupasco says, "The archetype on which Jung has rightly so firmly insisted, searching in it for the soul itself, testifies, in logical terms, that it is the state of contradiction that provokes the coexistence of homogeneity and heterogeneity. However, it should not be thought that in the so-called primitive peoples, as well as in the civilized, the psyche creates the mouth to escape from the historic and penetrate into the intemporal and eternal. The psyche engenders the myth as an irresistible emanation of its own constitution, which consists precisely of a conflict between the transcendental identity of the universality and invariability of the archetype and the heterogenizing temporality of the concrete situation in which he is incarnate."

23 *Time and Space*

At present, musicians must go through long years of professional training, in which no study is made of time except in a chronological sense. As long as they are restricted to chronological time, musicians can only produce a series of notes which add up but never generate themselves or pass into rhythm to make of the work they are singing or playing a totality potentially present in the sound images. The landscape of their musical training is homogeneous, since no alternative to chronological time is offered to them. This problem is not even contemplated, and rhythm itself is only considered in relation to chronological time. Furthermore, the silences they encounter in the musical score are felt as voids, empty spaces which break up the continuity and whose duration is hard to calculate. In complex works, the appearances of the several voices or instruments are known as entries, which implies, of course, a temporary absence, an interruption of their participation, ignoring that what the music has to communicate is transmitted as much through the silences as through the sounds.

To produce real music, musicians must cross the threshold of chronological time to set up a rhythmic flow of sound images (which include the silences) in sacred space-time in an eternal present here/now. They must situate themselves at the "intersection of the timeless with time" (T.S. Eliot). In order to do this they must have experienced and thus be able to discriminate between the two distinct qualities of time and space to which we will now refer.

Time is one of the greatest enigmas for the understanding of music and the activity of the musician. Time is an indispensable and inexplicable word which we use freely at any moment.

For some people it is a synonym of duration, of something which passes, a series of moments which add up. For them time is homogeneous and can be measured by the clock. The Occident has favored the production of men of action and enterprise for whom time is gold. To be always doing something is a maximum virtue and the contrary a sin. To meditate is to be idle, wasting one's time. The present-day interest in meditation is something exotic imported from the orient, but it responds to a basic need.

Some people live in a time fragmented into past, present and future. By a strange paradox, they live almost exclusively in the past and in the future. When they are not recalling the past with joy or bitterness, they are planning for themselves a golden future. In the present they are absent. If at any moment, in the midst of this vortex of action, they feel that time has stood still, it produces in them an emptiness where nothing happens and they fall into a mortal boredom. They then invent fresh activities to relieve their boredom. In this way they fall into an annihilating routine in which everything repeats itself.

The present is the fearful instant in which all time reintegrates into an eternal present and in which a person abandons action in order to *be*. It is the "straight and narrow" road of access to reality, to the sacred, to the mythic world of origins. To be present in the present signifies being in the presence of Being . . . a paradoxical situation. As T.S. Eliot tells us:

> *Men's curiosity searches past and future*
> *And clings to that dimension. But to apprehend*
> *The point of intersection of the timeless*
> *With time, is an occupation for the saint—*
> *No occupation either, but something given*
> *And taken, in a lifetime's death in love,*
> *Ardour and selflessness and self-surrender.*

> *For most of us, there is only the unattended*
> *Moment, the moment in and out of time,*
> *The distraction fit, lost in a shaft of sunlight,*
> *The wild thyme unseen, or the winter lightning*
> *Or the waterfall, or music heard so deeply*
> *That it is not heard at all, but you are the music*
> *While the music lasts.*

Ridiculous the waste sad time
Stretching before and after.

There exist, then, two completely different qualities of time: sacred and profane. Eliade says that the essential difference between these two qualities of time is this: sacred time is by nature reversible, in the sense that it is, properly speaking, a mythic primordial time become present. It is the experience of sacred time that allows the religious individual to reencounter periodically the Cosmos as it was at the beginning in the mythic instant of Creation. This religious nostalgia expresses one's desire to live in a pure and sanctified Cosmos, just as it was in the beginning when it was emerging from the hand of the Creation. This would explain why true music transmitted to us through this sacred eternal present has such a profound effect on us. It reinstates us momentarily and ontologically into the original mythical landscape of our being.

"Sacred time is indefinitely recuperable. From a certain point of view we could say that it does not 'pass' or constitute an irreversible duration. It is a purely ontological time, 'Parmenidean,' always equal to itself. It is unchanging and inexhaustible. For the non-religious individual, this transhuman quality of liturgical time is inaccessible. For profane man, time cannot present rupture or mystery; it constitutes the most profound existential dimension of a human being; it is related to its own existence, for it has a beginning and an end, which is death, the annihilation of existence. In comparison with religious man, there exists an essential difference: the *homo religiosus* experiences 'sacred' intervals that have no participation in the temporal duration that precedes and follows them; it has a totally different structure and origin, for it is a primordial time sanctified by the gods and able to become present through the medium or rite." The experience of music would be such an interval.

"For the *homo religiosus,* time and space are fused into a single entity. For him, neither time nor space are homogeneous nor continuous. Both partake of the same sacred, ontologic, incommensurable quality."

For us there exists an exterior and an interior space. Exterior space surrounds and contains us. This space is completely measurable and divisible. One can observe, describe and analyze it, but is not implicated in any way in it, nor do we assume any responsibility with regard to it. Interior space is boundless and incommensurable and can be of a psychological or of an ontological mythical quality.

And Ernst Cassirer *(An Essay on Man)* observes: "Mythic space is totally opposed to the empty formal space in which we situate our thought and activity. The space of traditional societies is not just a simple container, but an absolute space. It is not only rational and functional, a point of view of the spirit, but a structured space which has in all places a distinctive concrete qualification; not a dimension of dispersion, of pure and simple exteriority, but, on the contrary, a principle of reunion and totality, of implication between contain and contained."

Edmund Carpenter in *Eskimo* says: "We feel more comfortable when dealing with visible things; in this way it seems easier to us to understand, judge and maybe control them. In daily life, space is conceived in terms of that which separates visible objects. An empty space suggests somewhere where there is nothing to see. We say that a gasoline drum is empty when it is full of gases, or a tundra swept by gales. The Eskimo does not think in this way. I knew a hunter who, on being assured by a white man that a gasoline drum was empty, struck a match to look inside. He bears the scars for the rest of this life . . .

"The Eskimo do not separate time and space conceptually; they orient themselves simultaneously within both. Their idea of space is not that of something static and enclosed, but of a dynamic orientation. This factor appears in their language. Eskimo contains a quantity of words—*tima* (here/now), for example—that alone or as a suffix indicates orientation in time-space."

Mircea Eliade says that "on the contrary, for profane experience, space is homogeneous and neutral; no rupture distinguishes in quality the different parts of the mass. Geometric space can be marked and limited in every possible direction, but its own structure indicates no orientation or difference in quality. All true orientation disappears, because the 'still point' no longer enjoys a unique ontological status; it appears and disappears according to the necessities of daily life. The truth is that there no longer exists a 'world' but the fragments of a broken universe, an amorphous mass of an infinity of more or less neutral places in which man moves around under the dominion of the obligation of any existence integrated into an industrial society."

To this we will add the words of Gaston Bachelard: "Let us examine some very simple images, those which create a *happy space*. Our investigation, from this point of view, merits the name of topophilia. They attempt to determine the human value of possessed spaces, of the spaces defended against adverse forces, the loved spaces. For many reasons and the differences of the poetic shades of meaning, these are praised spaces. To their protective value, which can be positive, we must add their imagined values, which on the whole, are the dominant ones. The space upon which the imagination seizes cannot continue to be an indifferent one at the mercy of the measurement and reflection of the geometrician. It is a lived space. Lived, moreover, not in its positivity, but in all the partialities of the imagination." A very simple example would testify to the distinct qualities space can reveal: A is a rectangular plane, divisible and measurable. If I add to this space the smallest element of a different nature, it immediately changes its quality and is no longer divisible and measurable. The added element creates its own space.

A

B

If the music comes to us through a simultaneous projection of myth, symbol and image which evokes in us a profound ontological resonance, it is obvious that music can only come into existence in sacred space-time here/now.

24 *The Nature of Art*

Music is recognized as one of the modes of expression of art. Where did this term "art" come from? What is understood by art? It has come down to us across the centuries, bringing with it so many contradictory implications, confessed or not, that today it is no easy task to discern what is true and what is false. An inquiry is therefore necessary. Out of the jungle of possible present day testimonies, we will choose that of Susanne Langer (*The Problems of Art*).

> *Art is not a late addition to civilized life, a flowering of highly developed cultures, but something that is born during the first appearance and primitive stages of cultures; it is something that has often surpassed all other elements in achieving mature character and technical capacity. Cultures arise with the development of individual, social and religious sentiment, for which art is the perfect instrument.*
>
> *Art is the product of that spontaneous institution which is only given us in that state of ingenuous innocence which by its very nature excludes reflection, and to which only those who are still below it or already above it, those who have not yet reached it (like the child and members of traditional societies) or those who have left it behind them can have access.*
>
> *Art simply presents forms, which are often intangible to the imagination. The imagination is probably the oldest typically human mental trait, older than discursive reason; it is probably the common source of dream, reason, religion and all true observation. It is this primitive human power that engenders the arts and is at the same time affected by its products.*
>
> *Art is a certain vision of human sentiment incarnate in the work, sentiment which is not represented, but composed and*

155

articulated by the total apparition, the artistic symbol, im-
possible to find anywhere but there, directly through intuition,
impossible to demonstrate or to translate into discursive
language.

In the sense in which an artist speaks of "significant form,"
or "expressive form," it is not an abstracted form but an ap-
parition; and the vital processes of meaning and emotion that
good art expresses, for whoever is capable of perceiving them,
seem to be directly contained in the work, not symbolized, but
really represented. The congruence is so impressive that symbol
and meaning seem to constitute a single reality. In the same
way, the balanced forms, colors, lines and masses in good
painting, sculpture and architecture, have the aspect of emo-
tions, vital tensions and their resolutions. They present us with
forms for living.

Let us turn now to the Eskimos, contemporary members
of a traditional society as seen by Edmund Carpenter in *Eskimo.*

In the Eskimo language there exists no word for art or artist.
Art is everything well made and artist is any Eskimo. The
Eskimo makes no distinction between utilitarian and decorative
objects. They simply say, "The things that man makes must be
well made." My use of the words art and artist is strictly Occi-
dental. By art I mean objects that an Occidental critic would
consider artistic. Artist is any Eskimo.

Carving like singing is not something invented. "When you
feel a song within you, you sing it; when you feel a form emerge
from the ivory, you liberate it."

Whilst the carver holds the virgin ivory loosely in his hand,
turning it round and round, he murmurs, "Who are you? Who
is hiding there?" and then exclaims: "Ah! it is a seal."

They rarely propose to carve anything in particular. They
take the ivory and examine it in order to discover its occult form,
and if this does not appear immediately, they begin to carve aim-
lessly until they see it, accompanying themselves with liturgical
song while they work. Then they discover it. The hidden seal
emerges. It was always there. They had not created it; they liber-
ated it. They helped it to manifest itself.

*Car le créateur ou le poéte n'est point celui qui invente ou
d´montre, mais celui qui fait devenir.*

— Saint-Exupéry *La Citadelle*

*For the creator or the poet is not the one that invents or
demonstrates, but he who makes manifest.*

(Translation)

 *The Eskimo language has no words really equivalent to our
"create" and "make" which imply imposition of oneself. The
most approximate Eskimo word signifies "to work on" which
also involves an act of will, although restricted. The carver
never attempts to force the ivory into uncharacteristic forms, but
responds to the material which tries to be what it is; thus the
carving modifies itself continuously according to the demands of
the ivory.*

 *There have been Occidental artists who sometimes expressed
themselves and thought in this way, but they were exceptions
within their culture, arriving at this attitude individually, and
only after long experience and contemplation. The Eskimos, on
the contrary, learn it as their mother tongue and every day give
it social voice and expression. This is their attitude not only
towards the ivory, but towards everything, especially people:
parents and children, man and wife.*

 *We think of art as a possession and possession for us means
control, to handle as we please. For the Eskimo, art is a transi-
tory act, a relationship. They are more interested in the experience of creative activity than in the products of this activity.
These products are not collected or treasured or signed. On the
contrary, having passed around from hand to hand, they are
abandoned.*

 *The object is not contemplated artistically from a distance;
the carver penetrates it, he mingles and fuses himself with it. He
does not stand apart, contemplating and controlling, but participates in the essence of seal and walrus. This participation is not
limited to sight, for Aivilik Eskimo art does not reproduce the
visible, but makes things visible. It displays not only what is
perceived but also the true and the known, and as truth in-*

volves all the senses, tradition and imagination, it illuminates all knowledge.

The attitude of the Eskimo exactly coincided with our own in every aspect. What was important to us was not the product but the experience of revealing one of its infinite unforeseeable expressive forms. We had to be the music, participate in its essence.

The Eskimos, inhabiting an inhospitable and isolated land, managed to survive embedded in their sacred world until the twentieth century and the arrival of western civilization. Their destiny and trajectory from then on can hardly be more instructive for us, who, as children, have suffered this same uprooting from our first sacred world and its spontaneous attitude, gestures and mode of expression, by modern society's imposition of its profane acquired attitudes and compulsory schooling by professional adults. We have now forgotten and even deny our first world.

The Eskimo's stone carving was created and utilized by the Occidentals. They were the only ones who believed in it . . . that is, until recently. Now it also serves to identify the Eskimo himself. Having deprived him of his legitimate heritage, and even of all memory of it, we offer him a substitute which he willingly accepts, since no other is permitted. Thus he comes to take his place on the world stage alongside the North American Indian whose headdress comes out of the catalogue of the large stores and can be ordered by post; his dances he has learnt in Disneyland, and his philosophy of life from the hippies. He now knows no other identity, and when he is shown the real treasures of his culture, when he hears the old songs and hears the ancient words, he responds aggressively: "It's a lie! It's a lie! The white man's lie! Don't come telling me who I am and who my ancestors were! I know! . . ."

The ancient world of the Eskimo in which existed the contemporaneity of all time and an interpenetrated space is now a thing of the past. The new stone sculptures, each with its fixed base and angle of vision, are the result of all this and are therefore easier to appreciate for the Occidental art-lover.

In promoting the new sculptures in stone, the Canadian government has publicized the works and the names of certain expert carvers, a new concept, totally opposed to the anonymity of the aboriginal Eskimo art. The aboriginal carvers did not even attempt to develop a personal style and they had no interest in being remembered as individuals; they simply disappeared into the landscape of their works.

25 *Affectivity*

Perhaps one of the strangest and most intriguing aspects of our musical experience was the spontaneous flow of impersonal affectivity which united and sustained us when working, singing or playing together. It was not a personal affection for each other but something of quite a different nature, which everyone channeled but did not produce. It created a wordless communication and understanding between us at an ontological level. It also seemed to create a sacred space which still subsists. Strangers who knew nothing of our work, on coming into the large room of my house many years later, would sit down, relax and subside into a prolonged silence. Then they would tell me they had such a sensation of well-being that they felt they could sit there forever. "What is there so special about this room?" they would ask me.

This same affectivity characterized our attitude to the instruments we employed, and coincided exactly with that of Peiwoh who "with tender hand caressed the harp and softly touched the chords." It is only thus that a musician can produce the affective quality of musical sound.

Affectivity presents us with the greatest enigma of all, and we attempted to elucidate our own experience of it by exploring the studies of Stéphane Lupasco's *The Three Substances* and also his *New Aspects of Art and Science*.

> A strange idea comes into men's minds when they interrogate themselves about their soul, an idea which is self-sufficient, and a point which contains the clearest and most confusing characteristics of being; an idea whose nature has nothing in common with all that depends on one or other of the energy

161

systems or with the elements of "matter." These are essentially
relational; they never exist except in relation to something else:
this paper in relation to the table, for instance; an idea, then,
that cannot be considered homogeneous nor heterogeneous;
neither dynamic nor static; an idea which cannot essentially be
applied to anything else, and yet it contains us, penetrates us
and surrounds us everywhere: this is affectivity.

Affectivity poses the most difficult and the least studied of
all problems. We have examined it from one side and another in
our works. If energy knows and is known by virtue of the very
nature of its systems, in the last instance it only knows itself.
The ontological experience of affectivity seems to remain beyond
its cognitive possibilities, although it includes itself in them
mysteriously and capriciously.

We experience this singular substantiality, these noumenal
riches, *which bathe the delicate base of the soul, but we have no*
idea of why or how. This poses the most difficult problem of all:
the problem of being.

Affectivity is an enigma, mystery of mysteries, a kind of
senseless Grace. Affectivity simply is. *Affectivity is self-*
sufficing in its rigorously singular nature and refers only to
itself. It is ineffable and indefinable. Affectivity is in itself
unmoving; it imposes its presence under a thousand guises, no
doubt; there are presences which do not succeed but substitute
each other, since the affective is extra-temporal and extra-spatial.

Affectivity can only be, *and I can only experience it as it* is.
Affectivity is, in every sense of the word, an ontological fact.

The immense majority of the signals and information of the
biological system appear like those of a cybernetic machine; they
are more precise, rapid, automatic and efficacious and of such a
nature that they can do without this curious affectivity. In fact,
the greater part of our daily gestures and behavior is carried out
in this way. I avoid a blow, cross a street full of traffic, drive my
car, etc., . . . without the least display of sentiment of any kind.
The same thing occurs with our intellectual activities: I make
plans, combine things, calculate, learn, retain the most unpleas-
ant knowledge, remember . . . with the greatest of indifference.
And it would be easy to conceive a vital system that always
functioned in this way, in this complete peace; more, it is this

almost perfect affective void which usually introduces itself, more or less consciously, in this notion of peace.

But a play, music or a painting in which we contented ourselves with examining their technical procedures, intellectual significance, historic influences and their social and religious symbolism, etc., and which does not rouse in us the slightest emotion, would be non-existent.

What the artist attempts, what he is expected to do, is to awaken affectivity.

Is it affectivity that gives birth to the notion and term being *and not that affectivity has its origin in being? . . . This we cannot tell.*

If we remove from our world all traces of affectivity, nothing ontological is left. Even so, affectivity would continue to exist the same as ever and just as it is constituted. If, then, that which supports the characteristics of being reduces itself to affective data, if it is affectivity that is ontological and not the ontological which is affective, we find ourselves face to face with a transcendency which is a pure mystery. We cannot proceed any further.

Affectivity eludes time and the contingencies of past and future; it is purely present; the which is yet another proof of its ontological character. Our notions of absoluteness and eternity are doubtless dictated to us by our affective experience.

And as affectivity, although wrapped in the greatest mystery, oozes with a particular abundance over the energy systems in which the contradictory antagonism is richer and more intense, that is, the systems I have called neurophysical, we may well ask ourselves whether the notion of eternity and soul which has obsessed all men and all peoples does not take its origin from its affective contents.

Each one of us, moreover, possesses as a kind of perfume his own affective seal, which, in the last instance, would seem to characterize our uniqueness and substantial profundity, escaping the vicissitudes of uninterrupted transformations.

The last word shall be that of the poet.

With the drawing of this Love and the voice of this Calling
We shall not cease from exploration
And the end of all our exploring
Will be to arrive where we started
And know the place for the first time.
Through the unknown, remembered gate
When the last of earth left to discover
Is that which was the beginning;
At the source of the longest river,
The voice of the hidden waterfall
And the children in the apple-tree
Not known, because not looked for
But heard, half-heard, in the stillness
Between two waves of the sea.
Quick now, here, now, always—
A condition of complete simplicity
(Costing not less than everything)
And all shall be well and
All manner of thing shall be well
When the tongues of flame are in-folded
Into the crowned knot of fire
And the fire and the rose are one.

— T.S. Eliot *The Four Quartets*

26 *Music and Musicians*

We are now, I think, in a position to draw some conclusions from our own experiences and from those of other investigators. My chief concern here has been to bring them into contact in the hope that the interplay of multiple experience and research might throw a new light on the enigmas of music and music making. Most of the studies which I have cited are well known in their own fields, but seem never to have been taken into account as having any bearing on music and musicians.

At present the word *music* is used to indicate manifestations so heterogeneous and unlike each other, that it only serves to show confusion, disorientation and misunderstandings. We must, therefore, make a discriminating review of the situation.

Music belongs to the major field of art; it is, therefore, subject to the same exigencies as all works of real art. But here we find ourselves up against the same problem, for the word art is in the same situation as the word *music* . . . use and abuse has left it worn out and void of meaning. All we can do then is to retrace our steps to their origin in order to reactualize the primitive content of these terms.

The true work of art presents to us a living image which brings us into the presence of Reality. All the fields of art produce an enormous quantity of manifestations which lack artistic image. The artistic image is not constituted by the sounds, words or object represented. These are only a vehicle. The image is not a physical presence but a vibration which emanates and pervades everything.

The primary condition then, for a manifestation to be a work of art, is that it present an artistic image. In the case of music it must present us with a rhythmic flow of sound images. Images

are neither inert nor innocuous; they operate, resounding, con-
voking, claiming our presence and participation. But there are
two classes of images:

A.   Those which emerge from the world of imagination and
orient us towards the immobile Center and sanity, and connect us
with Reality.

B.   Those which arise from a world of hallucination and orient
us towards disease, madness and death.

The first call and orient us towards the One, the still point,
the Being who is beyond all contingent activity. They have a
mythic, symbolic and archetypal content which operates to
connect us with life and health.

The second convoke us at physical, biological and psychic
levels to the great contingent activity of the homogeneous and the
heterogeneous, leading to disease, chaos and death. In our present day society, images of the second type prevail. They assail us
everywhere through our ears and eyes, from all sides and at
every moment, affecting children and adults alike.

Real music projects in us the first type of images. It breaks
into our daily context as something completely different, as the
apparition of the Sacred and of Meaning. In our profane world of
illusion and absurdity, it therefore appears with the quality of
hierophany.

The sound images, bearers of *hierophany,* emerge from a
rhythmic flow of sound which creates the symbolic form of their
content. Rhythm is a vital breath which flows sonorously through
an eternal present to create "form." Rhythm is another word
worn out by use and abuse. Music students are taught that
rhythm is an organized succession of fractions of chronological
time. This is an aberration since in chronological time, differentiated sounds can only accumulate, they cannot fuse to constitute a
rhythmic form.

In the sacred present, the only instant in which real music
can appear, rhythm is an indivisible flow of sound creating form
through a process of genesis. Sounds are inextricably united
because they are born of each other. Here sounds do not separate
in order to affirm their identity; they integrate into a timeless
mythic landscape. From there they engender images which offer
us forms for living.

The constituent material of music, sound, is neither inert nor innocuous, but a primordial energy, creator and destroyer of form. How different the human climate in which we now live would be if only humanity would remember this fundamental fact, for then we should only produce sounds that are really musical. This alone would change the face of the earth and man's health. At present we are submerged in a world of un-musical sound, a situation of which few people are aware or care.

For not all sounds are musical or apt for musical purposes, and only the inner musical ear, the "fine ear," as St. Bernard calls it, can discriminate between the musical and the un-musical sound. Musical sound is a direct channel through which reality makes itself present. For this reason, musical sound must be a good conductor, resonant, buoyant, transparent and imbued with affectivity.

The formative basis of the musician must be singing . . . not professional, but spontaneous singing with a natural voice which arises in everyone as a vital expressive necessity. For singing, the student must be provided with an ample and varied repertory of traditional songs from all lands, children's songs and nursery rhymes, singing games and dances, work songs, love songs and above all romances and ballads. On this basis the chorales of Bach can then be incorporated as a first experience of harmony and polyphony, works for several voices from any epoch from the Middle Ages onwards, arias, and lieder. A great number of professional musicians don't sing, and their speaking voice is unmusical.

Music students must begin by *singing* and producing with their own voices, in a propitious attitude, sounds that are really musical. They must sing to and for themselves, and also in unison with others. The nefarious custom of selecting voices amongst students for singing, with the pretext that only some of them have a "good voice" and sing in tune, has silenced a large proportion of the population for the rest of their lives. Real musical singing is the most natural and direct mode that human beings have of praying and maintaining their connection with reality, and ontological affectivity. To deprive them of this possibility is to mutilate them. Everyone has a voice unless they were born mute, and I know from long years of experience with children, juveniles and adults that by singing together in unison, everybody soon sings in tune. All songs must be learnt by ear; later the students can use the score of the songs they know well and have assimilated. Whatever instrument a student plays, it must "sing" from the very start. For this to be possible, students must transfer to their instrument the experience of expressing themselves musically with their voices.

Real musical sound requires an intense interior silence with which to come into play. Such a silence is not easy to achieve in the times we live in. Furthermore, human beings have psychological reasons for rejecting it. Ouspensky, the Russian mathematician and psychologist, calls our attention to a voice we all have inside us, which talks incessantly with an unrestrainable, mechanical verbosity. This voice, which usually bewails our fate, makes us waste our time and finer energies in considering and passing judgement. It stirs up in us an extensive scale of emotions; at the end of the day we are exhausted without knowing why. It is this voice which inspires our suffering and illusions. Ouspensky adds that the last thing we are willing to renounce is our suffering, for it is a common way of claiming attention and affection. It is impossible to silence this voice for more than a second. The best way to silence it is to substitute for it, put something else in its place. In my own experience, working with students and with myself, when human beings are nourished with songs of authentic musical value, it is these that flow continually within them, supplanting the verbosity. They carry out for us a function analogous to that of the prayer wheel in the hands of Tibetan monks. These songs, instead of exhausting us, nourish us and keep us oriented towards the Center; they give us peace, security and plentitude even amidst the most extreme contingencies of life.

In the world of musical activity, both in teaching and performance, it is unusual for the quality of sound to be given the decisive importance it merits. At this moment, the majority of musical instruments in use are mass produced without the intervention of musicians. Perhaps the instruments that have suffered most are the piano and the organ. The makers pay great attention to the demands of the market, and what the market asks of them at the moment is a brilliant, hard, heavy, strident and aggressive sound that distorts and extinguishes its natural resonances . . . and this is what they produce. The so-called concert instruments have become luxury articles owing to their inaccessible prices, but even these conform to public taste. The makers have flooded the market with more economic instruments intended for students from which it is impossible to obtain a musical sound. All music students must have an instrument capable of producing musical sound from the outset, otherwise they will become musically deaf. There is no reason why a really musical instrument should be an article of luxury. It is impossible to make music with unmusical sounds. A healthy reaction is to be observed all around in the emergence of luthiers mostly interested in the individual construction of old instruments. The human voice is the most intimate and delicate of all instruments and is a true reflection of the quality of the performer.

Another serious problem afflicting music at present is the continual rise in pitch of the international A. In the course of my lifetime, it has risen nearly 3/4 of a tone. As a consequence, the works are sung and played in higher keys than the composers intended, giving them a degree of nervous and emotional tension that was not in the original. It is as if we transported a painting to a brighter scale of colors; the original changes into something different. Perhaps the instrument most affected by this is the voice.

The written or printed score is inoperative until there appears a human being capable of sonorizing and reactualizing it. And here we come to a crucial problem, for to possess the title of musician does not necessarily mean that you are one. In oral tradition, gesture and sound image were fused into a single expressive manifestation. The same is not true of written music. At present it is possible to possess a great musical erudition and a technique that makes possible a brilliant performance without being a musician or having any notion of what it's all about. Such a situation is the result of an absurd unmusical training. Students after long years of technical-intellectual training to ensure a correct, literal rendering of the score, have deafened their inner musical ears and put their capacity to create and perceive images out of action. With such a preparation, it is impossible to cross the threshold of music, because it does not prepare the student to pass from chronological into sacred time-space in which to establish a rhythmic flow of sound images imbued with a profound symbolic content.

The ear which has not developed its capacity to create and perceive images, only hears the notes, concrete individual sounds that do not transcend their condition as such. In the same way the eye which is unable to read by image only sees concrete objects. Looking at a Gothic cathedral or a Romanesque church, all it sees is a mass of stones architecturally organized. The diffusion of literacy is of very recent date. Before this we were all thrown back on our natural capacity to read by image and perceive the meaningful content of what we saw and heard. Our books were the infinite variety of images that presented themselves to our eyes and ears, especially in Nature.

If real musicians are to appear on the scene, then obviously what is needed is a radical revision of the student's preparation; it must be formative and creative and lay aside all advertised methods which are only concerned with the outer ear and eye. When methods are applied, teaching can be neither musical nor creative, since what matters is the success of the method, not the development of each individual's musicality.

The exterior (optic) eye and the acoustic exterior can only recognize, analyze and differentiate, and for this very reason they are inadequate for perceiving the image which is not present in the score or in the visual landscape. The image is a subtle vibration which the inner eye and the inner musical ear capture by coming into resonance with it.

The real task of the musician is the reactualization of the creation of a universe of sound which starts with the first sound that breaks the silence. From then on, sound and silence are inextricably fused into a ying-yang through which meaning is transmitted. The musician's inner ear and attention must always be focused on the birth and quality of each individual sound, not on the notes.

Perhaps one of the most disorienting terms in common musical usage is *interpretation*, for it induces us to believe that the function of the musician is to interpret something. As to what this "something" is, there exist innumerable theories that have nothing to do with reality. The function of musicians is just the opposite: they must make of themselves a channel for a flow of sound images. These images arise in the measure of their inner obedience to the expressive demands of a Reality which makes itself present and manifest. Their task is not to intervene, but to give a faithful response to these significant stimuli . . . action through no-action. For them to be able to accomplish this, they must be free of all exterior pressure and direction, and of all theories and preconceptions with reference to the version of the work which is about to appear, for this must be original and therefore unforeseeable.

In the present panorama of the professional world of music perhaps we could find a paradigmatic model, as far as his gesture is concerned, in von Karajan, who, the instant he begins a concert, would seem to turn his attention inward to place body, mind and soul at the disposal of the music, transforming himself into one more instrument of the orchestra, thus giving the musicians freedom of expression.

My own experience has taught me that under these conditions (and even dispensing with a conductor) there results an expressive unity and a live rhythmic flow, impossible to attain by any other means. In this way, each version of the work comes fresh, unforeseeable, original, unique, and unrepeatable from the hands and voices of true musicians.

I possess an old recording of Bach's *Mass in B Minor*, made by von Karajan. It contains an extraordinary version of the Crucifixus obtained in this way. The orchestral chords fall on the ear like lashes of a whip, marking with implacable precision the passage of chronological time which crucifies and kills us. Only when they come to "passus et sepultus est" do these chords submerge themselves into an a temporal rhythmic flow, there to subside into silence.

Naturally such a gesture of total submission and strict inner obedience cannot be improvised. For us who have been taught to read and write and have been brought up in a materialistic and intellectualized society, it implies a long process of unflagging inner culture in order to liberate and develop our innate creative and imaginative capacity. But if this gesture is lacking, neither real music, nor a real musician can appear. It is a gesture that is not limited to musical experience but implicates the individual's whole vision of life.

Illiterate peoples, who retain their traditions, whether they belong to a prehistoric culture, or rural community, have maintained this innate creative and imaginative capacity in general use. The richness and originality of their creations bear witness to this; they are not the work of professionals but of everybody. They create very powerful images with the simplest ordinary materials. We reactualized this experience by recreating the Bayeux Tapestry. Japanese craftsmen, when creating the temple garden, use a minimum of natural elements: stones, trees, water, flowers, bamboo. But they dispose them in such a way that individually and collectively they transform themselves into *hierophanies*. A stone garden can be more eloquent and instructive than a whole library, if the one who contemplates it can read by image.

It might be opportune to cite here some observations of Lewis Thomas (*The Lives of a Cell*): "Since everything else that we recognize as human behavior derives from the central mechanism of language, the same sets of genes are at least indirectly responsible for governing such astonishing behavior as in the concert hall, where hundreds of people crowd together, silent, head-tilting, meditating, listening to music as though receiving instructions."

When music and musicians accomplish their real function, the result is a *hierophany*. The work, the performers, and the listeners disappear, all submerged in an eternal present, in the flow of cosmic affectivity which emanates from Being. The ontological experience of being a coparticipant in this present nourishes, vitalizes and orients us. The musicians, through the music, have reactualized the sonorous cosmogony and propitiated a paradisiac state of plentitude.

That real music is a *hierophany*, a momentary apparition of the sacred within the profane context of our daily lives, is something which has long been forgotten by our modern, industrialized society. This society is more interested in what people can produce than in what they are and experience. Life in general, human beings in particular, are evaluated in terms of utility: saleable services and commodities. It is a society that, in spite of its many brilliant achievements, has become dangerously ill, and is sliding rapidly towards chaos and insanity owing to erroneous modes of life. These suppress creative, imaginative and transcendental experience, myth and inner spiritual development free of all sectarism and dogmas.

Doctors are impotent to turn the tide and restore us to spiritual health, for what they have to deal with are the effects produced by the lack of ontological affectivity and security. It is this affectivity which nourishes being and promotes life and health; it is impersonal, gratuitous and atemporal. It has nothing to do with personal, passionate affection. By adopting a profane mode of life, the modern world has cut itself adrift from the affectivity of Being so effectively that countless human beings are now living as isolated orphans in a senseless disintegrated universe in which they have no place, function or meaning.

What doctors cannot achieve, musicians can, but we must first create them. This would necessarily involve a radical change of criterion with regard to musical education. A true musician can reconnect us with the experience of ontological affectivity, while awakening and bringing into play our innate wisdom and musicality; this is achieved through the resonant impact of significant sound images and the experience of making them. Music is the quickest, most direct and efficacious way of reincorporating us into the mythical landscape of our lives, the experience of which lifts us momentarily out of the devastating conflictive contingencies of a profane existence into the beatific plentitude of being. This gives us a point of reference by which to orient ourselves. For a brief moment we experience what all humans secretly long for: a return to the Garden of Eden, to that primordial state of peace, freedom and affective at-oneness which is our birthright, but is usually deemed utopian and even impossible to achieve in this world.

Music is a means, not an end, and true musicians are capable of transforming themselves into a resonant musical instrument on which Reality can play.

Millions of students go through music schools; there, teaching is aimed at concert performance. Of these students, very few ever reach a concert platform, either locally or internationally. So we are left with an army of frustrated performers, who mostly go into teaching to earn a living. Having no real comprehension either of music or of teaching, they simply teach as they were taught, aiming once again at concert performance.

I have been very interested to see how some of my students, who worked with me for many years, gradually became absorbed into various professions and activities, maintaining the true musician's attitudes as a basis for their work which thereby acquired a distinctive quality. Some of them are teachers at our elementary school. None of them has developed a strong personality, but working intensely in silence and anonymity they have achieved an original creative and healthy individuality. By striving to live musically and obey the dictates of their innate wisdom, they have become a silent but efficacious point of reference and existential orientation for others. We all of us hope for a better world, but usually forget that we are the constituents and the makers of whatever world exists. If the fact of the earth is to be changed, it is we who must change. This is the most and the only thing we can do. Musical experience is the most direct and efficacious way of reorienting ourselves towards becoming real human beings. In this lifelong effort, as T.S. Eliot reminds us, we are not defeated only because we keep on trying.

I am convinced that far more important than aiming at a concert platform to gain personal fame and applause, musicians' true role is that of Parsifal in a sick community—they should awaken in themselves and in others the "fine" inner ear, intimately connected with our capacity for survival. Spontaneous singing should become once again an essential part of daily life for all human beings, and it is the musicians' task to provide us with adequate material and opportunity.

Just as the musical principle of resonance seems to be active in establishing order and unity in a spontaneously creative universe, so the resonances set up in the making and experience of real music could help to unite humanity into a significant spiritual whole with a common creative purpose: the individual attainment of peace, freedom and the affectivity of being. Music can reorient life towards a plentitude of being which transcends all the temporal, material passions and illusions which now divide and devour it. It can open for us the door to immortality.

True musicians have a decisive role to play in turning the tide of humanity's madness and despair, and it is urgent that they assume it by making of themselves and the music they produce a *hierophany*.

What we call the beginning is often the end
And to make an end is to make a beginning.
The end is where we start from.

— T.S. Eliot *The Four Quartets*

The Contributions of Other Investigators

Into this warp of permanent musical experience of which I have given a brief account, we had been weaving the multicolored threads provided by those investigating in the same or other fields . . . philosophy, history of religions, psychology, physics, biology, philology, poetry, medicine, anthropology and art. Of all the available material, I selected those which seemed to throw the strongest light on our own experience.

Joseph Campbell   — *The Hero with a Thousand Faces*
Pantheon Books, New York, 1949

Mircea Eliade   — *The Sacred and the Profane*
Harcourt Brace, New York, 1959
— *Images and Symbols*
Sheed and Ward, New York, 1961

T.S. Eliot   — *The Four Quartets*
Harcourt Brace, New York, 1943

Herbert Larcher   — *L'architecture cistercienne*

Levy-Bruhl   — *The Primitive Mentality*
The Macmillan Company,
New York, 1923

Georges Gusdorf   — *Speaking*
Northwestern University Press, 1945
— *Mythe et Métaphysique*
Flammarion, Paris, 1953

Lewis Thomas   — *The Lives of a Cell*
Viking Press, New York, 1974

Edmund Carpenter   — *Eskimo Realities*
Holt Rinehart and Winston,
New York, 1973

James Halliday   — *Psychosocial Medicine*
Norton, New York, 1948

E. Cassirer   — *An Essay on Man*
Oxford University Press, 1944

G. Bachelard   — *The Poetics of Space*
Orion Press, New York, 1964

St. John of the Cross   — *The Poems of St. John of the Cross*
Grove Press, New York, 1959

Idris Shah   — *Tales of the Dervishes*
Dutton, New York, 1969

Ivan Illich   — *Awareness*

Marius Schneider   — *El espíritu de la música como origen del símbolo*
Revista Diógenes No. 27, p. 49-78, Buenos Aires, 1959
— *Encyclopedie de la Musique*
Gallimard

Stéphane Lupasco   — *Las Tres Materias*
Editorial Sudamericana, Buenos Aires, 1963

Albert Gleizes   — *La forme et l'histoire*
Jaques Povolozky, Paris, 1932

W.H. Hudson   — *Green Mansions*
Random House, 1944
— *The Purple Land*
Duckworth and Co., London, 1929

Susanne Langer   — *The Problems of Art*
Scribner, New York, 1957

Plato   — *Dialogues*
Pantheon Books, New York, 1961
Phaedrus